You have ju~~st~~ ... and Feng ~~Shui~~ ...

You've made ...~~great investment~~ in your future and you'll love the specialized insights on what to expect in terms of love, business, wealth and career in 2010!

But wait! Don't' Stop Here… There's More!

Now you can discover other powerful feng shui secrets from Lillian Too that go hand-in-hand with the valuable information you will find in this book.

And it's ABSOLUTELY FREE!

LILLIAN TOO's
NEW Online Weekly Ezine FREE!

You've taken the first step by purchasing this book. Now expand your wealth, luck and knowledge and sign up immediately! Just go to www.lilliantoomandalaezine.com and register today!

It's EASY! It's FREE! It's FRESH & NEW!

Don't Miss Out! Be one of the first to register at
www.lilliantoomandalaezine.com

Lillian's NEW Online FREE Weekly Ezine is only available to those who register online at
www.lilliantoomandalaezine.com

LILLIAN TOO & JENNIFER TOO

FORTUNE & FENG SHUI

OX

2010

Fortune & Feng Shui 2010 OX
by Lillian Too and Jennifer Too
© 2010 Konsep Lagenda Sdn Bhd

Text © 2010 Lillian Too and Jennifer Too
Design and illustrations © Konsep Lagenda Sdn Bhd

The moral right of the authors to be identified as authors of this book
has been asserted.

Published by KONSEP LAGENDA SDN BHD (223 855)
No 11A, Lorong Taman Pantai 7, Pantai Hills
59100 Kuala Lumpur, Malaysia

For more Konsep books, go to www.konsepbooks.com
or www.lillian-too.com.
To report errors, please send a note to errors@konsepbooks.com.
For general feedback, email feedback@konsepbooks.com.

ISBN 978-967-329--027-7
Published in Malaysia, July 2009

for more on all the recommended
feng shui cures, remedies & enhancers for

2010
please log on to

www.wofs.com/2010

and

www.fsmegamall.com

YEARS OF THE OX

Birth Year	Western Calendar Dates	Age	Kua Number Males	Kua Number Females
Wood Ox	24 Jan 1925 to 12 Feb 1926	85	3 East Group	3 East Group
Fire Ox	11 Feb 1937 to 30 Jan 1938	73	9 East Group	6 West Group
Earth Ox	29 Jan 1949 to 16 Feb 1950	61	6 West Group	9 East Group
Metal Ox	15 Feb 1961 to 4 Feb 1962	49	3 East Group	3 East Group
Water Ox	3 Feb 1973 to 22 Jan 1974	37	9 East Group	6 West Group
Wood Ox	20 Feb 1985 to 8 Feb 1986	25	6 West Group	9 East Group
Fire Ox	7 Feb 1997 to 27 Jan 1998	13	3 East Group	3 East Group

You are an OX born if your birthday falls between the above dates

Contents

OVERVIEW OF THE TIGER YEAR 2010

The Golden Tiger Year of 2010 reflects the character of the Tiger – an aggressive, fierce and tough year that is also resilient and with hidden good fortune possibilities. This Tiger Year is one of discordant energies. There are obstacles and frustrations ahead due to clashing elements, and the aggressive nature of the Tiger Year makes things worse. We face a scenario lacking in good signs; several traditional indicators suggest a challenging and difficult year. For many animal signs, 2010 is a time of tough choices and hard circumstances. For the Ox born, the Tiger year saps your energy although not enough to block your success luck, which is good.

Tiger Years bring out the best in many people. Forced to overcome strenuous situations, many rise to the challenge and as a result, those who think positive, act decisively and bring creative inputs into their work will see their efforts bearing fruit.

For the Ox born, the year promises good success but little in the way of financial rewards. If you can maintain good health and create strong energy, you can end the year better than when you start.

The Golden Tiger Year does not bring smooth sailing; but if you can stay resilient, you can successfully transform the year's problems into opportunities. It is vital not to get mentally defeated by the energy and feng shui afflictions of the year. The Ox understands it is better to recognize their essence and subdue them. Cures and remedies should be effectively applied. The coming twelve months from February 4th 2010 to February 4th 2011 will test the most resilient of professionals, and the most positive amongst us. The Year of the Ox just passed has been relatively stable but nevertheless fragile. The year of the Tiger is less stable, and conditions for work and business will be more difficult.

This is a year when the elements clash directly – the Metal of the year's heavenly stem destroys the Tiger's intrinsic Wood. Superficially, this is not a good sign. Yet Metal, when used with skill and under special circumstances, can transform Wood into something of great value. So even as Metal destroys Wood, it can transform Wood into an object of value. This is the hidden worth which all of us should strive to capture this year.

With the elements of the year clashing, hostilities can get ugly, competition nasty and the environment more hostile. Heaven and Earth energy are not in sync. It is left to mankind to use our creativity and prowess to rise to the year's challenges and emerge triumphant.

Natural luck is in short supply. But this does not mean we cannot create our own luck! The year's outlook simply manifest the way the elements of the year have arranged themselves – as revealed in the Paht Chee chart, and in the Flying Star feng shui charts of 2010. These charts have proved accurate in past years and are worth analyzing.

Note however that while the elements of the year influence the way luck manifests on a macro level, it is at the micro levels that an individual's luck is determined; and your elements at the micro level can be enhanced or subdued, can be transformed and made better. Here is where understanding astrological indications and feng shui can be so helpful.

There are ways to overcome negative energies caused by the clash of elements brought by missing elements, made worse by visiting "stars" of the 24 mountains or affected by elements that are hidden in the paht chee chart of the year. The "afflictions" we

have to confront in the Year of the Tiger, or in any
year, can all be remedied.

Remedial Actions

We can create elements that are missing; replenish
those that are in short supply; subdue misfortune
stars and activate positive stars that bring good
fortune to any home. This is the feng shui aspect
of corrective work that can be done to improve the
prosperity potential of your home.

The luck of individuals can also be improved by using
element astrology and this is laid out in detail in
the section on Annual Element Horoscopes, which
explain how the different elements of the Tiger Year
affects you based on your animal sign of the Ox and
your stem element. This year we also offer suggested
remedies. You can examine the pluses and minuses of
your horoscopes to improve your luck for the year. You
can use our suggestions and take steps to minimize
whatever horoscope obstacles afflict your sign.

Determine the elements that are missing or weak in
your birth horoscope. Note what elements require
replenishment; take note of particular afflictions that
can cause you the most problems. Then subdue them.
Your animal sign outlook changes from year to year,
so it is important to update.

Four Pillars Ruling the Year

PAHT CHEE CHART 2010 - YEAR OF THE GOLDEN TIGER

HOUR	DAY	MONTH	YEAR
HEAVENLY STEM 己 YIN EARTH	**HEAVENLY STEM** 乙 YIN WOOD	**HEAVENLY STEM** 戊 YANG EARTH	**HEAVENLY STEM** 庚 YANG METAL
EARTHLY BRANCH 乙 卯 RABBIT WOOD	**EARTHLY BRANCH** 辛 酉 ROOSTER METAL	**EARTHLY BRANCH** 甲 寅 TIGER WOOD	**EARTHLY BRANCH** 甲 寅 TIGER WOOD
HIDDEN HEAVENLY STEMS OF THE YEAR			
YIN WOOD	YIN METAL	YANG EARTH YANG WOOD YANG FIRE	YANG EARTH YANG WOOD YANG FIRE
The year is desperately short of WATER			

The year's ruling four pillars chart (illustrated below) shows there is an excess of **Wood element**, led by the Tiger whose intrinsic element is Yang Wood. Tiger appears twice, in the Year and in the Month Pillars, making its influence and that of the Wood element very strong. Note also that another **Yin wood** is brought by the Rabbit. So there are three wood branches in the chart. These are supplemented by yet another wood, i.e. the Yin Wood stem of the

Day pillar, making a total appearance of **four Wood elements in the chart**. The intrinsic element of the year is therefore **Strong Yin Wood**. This excess of the Wood element suggests a year fraught with competitive pressures, when even friends can become devious in the interests of surviving through tough times.

But the Wood element will get depleted. Two Earth elements symbolically distract Wood, and two Metal elements destroy Wood. This would have been fine, even auspicious, if the Wood element was being renewed by the presence of Water. The chart however is missing Water (and missing Fire). The Wood of the year thus signifies dead and dying wood that cannot grow. With crucial elements missing, expansion and productivity is greatly strained this year. The work scenario is tough!

Unbalanced Chart

With two elements missing and with too much Wood, the chart is considered unbalanced. This is not an auspicious sign. The presence of both yin and yang pillars makes up for this imbalance to some extent as neither positive yang nor negative yin energies dominate.

Two Metal in the chart suggests that power and rank come into focus during the year. There is no lack of leadership or mentor luck, and there is both yang as well as yin metal, male and female. Powerful men and women play a big role in the promise of the year's outlook.

Two Earth elements in the 2010 chart signify the presence of wealth luck. There is more wealth luck this year than last year. So despite an imbalance of elements in the chart, prosperity luck is present. This means there are opportunities for making money during the year.

What is needed to actualize wealth in 2010 is Water. It is only when the year's Wood element can flourish, grow and bring itself to fruition that money can be made. Wood needs Water, which is missing; WATER must thus be created!

The missing Water is significant. In addition, Fire is also missing. Without Water there can be no growth luck, and without Fire, there is no creativity! In the chart, the Fire element symbolizes ingenuity, intelligence, strategic thinking and mental clarity. Without clear foresight and creativity, the year lacks the spark to get things moving.

Those wishing to succeed must generate the **Fire element** within their living space, or personify this

element by wearing shades of the Fire element –
red. Only then will you be resourceful enough to
forge ahead. What is needed this year is vision and
imagination. If you can think of original ways of
moving ahead in your career, you will benefit greatly.

Hidden Elements

Since the year suffers from missing elements, we
examine if there are any hidden elements in the
chart. Usually, earthly branches always have hidden
heavenly stems and in 2010, the three animals of the
year; i.e. Tiger, Rooster and Rabbit, bring additional
elements that supplement the year's luck further. The
Tiger hides yang Earth, yang Wood and yang Fire
in the chart, and since Tiger appears twice, there are
two hidden Yang Fire. This suggests hidden creativity,
resourcefulness and ingenuity, as a result of which,
the year benefits. This is a good sign. And since Fire
exhausts Wood, its hidden presence will also subdue
competitive pressures.

However, there is no sign of hidden Water!

This serious lack of water means that although the
essence of the year is **Strong Wood**, missing Water
suggests rotting and depleting wood. It is hard to
accumulate asset wealth in 2010. Those of you who
create a powerful water feature in your work or living

space are sure to benefit. Water is what brings excellent feng shui to the year.

Crouching Tiger Hidden Dragon

A significant observation of the Paht Chee chart this year is the presence of the **Rabbit** which belongs to the Wood element, same as the **Tiger**. The two animals are symbols of Spring, and when combined with the **Dragon**, a trinity of animal signs get created that produces a very strong seasonal combination of Spring. These three animals rule the East and their combined strength is enormously empowering, especially as their presence is conducive to creating auspicious new beginnings!

The good news is that the Crouching Tiger can cause the Hidden Dragon to surface.

This is the source of the well known phrase "Hidden Dragon, Crouching Tiger" made so famous by the Ang Lee directed movie of the same name.

And since the Month Pillar of the year's chart has yang Earth, this is the ingredient required for the Dragon to rise from the ground and to fly magnificently into the skies. If this energy can be simulated, the Dragon creates the precious breath that brings good luck. It is thus significant that there is also the presence of the Rooster in the chart, as the Rooster is the Dragon's secret friend! The Rooster symbolizes the Phoenix enticing the Dragon to make an appearance!

Essential water in the East

The paht chee chart of the year has the ingredients required to generate the auspicious presence of the Dragon! It is thus extremely auspicious to invite the Dragon image into your home in 2010.

The Dragon is the celestial creature that will bring great good fortune to the year. Place a water feature with images of the crouching Tiger, hidden Dragon and the Rabbit in the East sector of the home.

In 2010, the East is visited by the heavenly star of 6 which brings good fortune. Placing Water in the East not only activates the luck of a good Spring, it also makes up for the lack of a *lap chun* caused by the lunar year starting late. The key to creating good energy for 2010 is thus a Dragon/Tiger/Rabbit water feature in the East!

The wearing of any kind of precious or semi-precious earth stone or of any kind of Dragon jewellery is especially meaningful in 2010. The stone signifies Earth which brings wealth luck, while the Dragon activates the luck of new beginnings, transforming the year's Tiger energy to work powerfully in your favor. The Dragon keeps the mighty fierce Tiger under control! This naturally favors the Ox, as it means the Tiger then becomes less dangerous.

Auspicious & Dangerous Stars

In 2010, two potentially auspicious stars and two potentially dangerous stars make an appearance. Both types of stars are powerful in their beneficial and malefic influences respectively. The two lucky stars bring good fortune; they impact different animal signs differently and in varying degrees, but they are generally beneficial.

1. Mentor Star

In Chinese astrology, much is made of "mentor" luck, which in the old days was a major factor bringing career success. This suggests there is patronage luck available to the younger generation. If you are working towards clear cut career goals, you can attract mentor luck. You can find powerful benefactors, and in 2010, success comes from "who you know rather than what you know." This star is also referred to as the "Heavenly Virtue Star". With its presence in the chart, it indicates help from powerful people. To activate this star, use the **Double Six Big Smooth Amulet** comprising six large coins laid out in a row. This amulet is fabulous for Ox-born people!

2. Star of Prospects

This favorable star brings a special energy that rewards determination and staying power. Those who have a passion for success will benefit from its presence. There is nothing that cannot be achieved for those prepared to work hard. Here we see ambition playing a big role in making the best of what the

The Star of Prospects brings success to those with determination and ambitions. It rewards those who are focused.

year brings. To activate this star, make sure you have a **Rabbit image** in the water features placed in your home. If you wish, you can also place a **Rat spouting jewels** near the water!

3. Aggressive Sword Star

This star is brought by the Tiger and there being two Tigers, it suggests that the Aggressive Sword's negative effects comes with a double whammy. This star brings fierce, ruthless and violent chi energy. People will push ahead at the expense of others using fair means or foul. The name of this star is *Yang Ren*, which describes a yang essence sharp blade that inflicts damage. This star has great potential for good or bad to materialize during the year, but is more negative than positive. The excess Wood in the year's chart makes things worse.

To be protected from falling victim to this star's aggressive influence, wear the **Double Ring Talisman**. Also excellent for overcoming the ferocity of the Aggressive Sword Star are the **Trinity Ring** and

Wear the Trinity Ring with mantra to protect yourself against the Star of Aggressive Sword. This Trinity Ring also signifies the trinity of *tien ti ren* - which is very auspicious.

pendants signifying heaven, earth and mankind chi. These come with powerful mantras of the Lotus Family of Buddhas – Amitabha, Chenrezig and Manjushuri.

Finally, a third remedy is the **Fire Magic Wheel** for those who may be especially badly hit by the year's fierce Tiger energy. If you find yourself falling ill a lot or suffering big doses of bad luck and disappointments, any one of these amulets are powerful ways to repel the bad luck.

4. Flower of Romance Star (External)
This is sometimes confused with the *Peach Blossom Star* because it addresses the destiny of love. When the flower of romance is present in any year, it suggests love blossoms easily between people but it is not the kind of love that leads to marriage and family; it indicates instead the possibility of extra-marital affairs bringing stress to happily married couples.

There is a difference between internal romance and external romance, and in the Year of the Tiger, it is the latter rather than the former that prevails. So the year will see increased occurrences of infidelity.

In 2010, the Rabbit in the Hour Pillar is the romance star of the Tiger, and because Rabbit occurs in the Hour Pillar, it signifies the *external romance star* and this makes all marriages vulnerable. Things are made worse by the Rooster in the Day Pillar, as Rooster clashes with Rabbit. This causes misunderstandings, although for the most part, infidelity in 2010 will not lead to divorce.

For the Ox wanting to protect your marriage from the *star of external flower of romance*, place the image of the **Rooster** either in the East of your room, or in your own direction of NE. The most vulnerable months for you are March and also January 2011 as these are the months when there could be infidelity temptations.

Placing a Rooster in the East will help protect against marriage infidelities this year.

Year's Feng Shui Chart

The luck of the year is also influenced by the year's feng shui chart, which reveals lucky and unlucky sectors of buildings, houses and apartments. The chart comprises a 3 x 3 sector grid of numbers that reveal the luck distribution of the year. 2010's chart is explained in detail in Part 4 of this book.

The fortune-bringing stars of the 24 mountains also affect the luck of the different sectors of your living space. The Fortune Stars add important nuances to what is revealed in the annual chart, and their combined influences also affect the luck of each individual animal sign. There are 108 different Fortune Stars, but only a handful fly into each of the 24 mountain directions in any year. These bring auspicious or harmful influences, but they vary in strength and type each year. The 24 Mountain Stars affect houses and animal signs equally. Some stars bring good luck, some bring misfortune, while others bring protection. When your sign is negatively afflicted and your vitality gets weakened, you need to wear specific protective Taoist charms. When your energy is heightened, the stars help you manifest whatever good fortune comes your way. These are explained in detail for your sign in Part 5 of the book.

Monthly Readings for the Whole Year

For the Ox, do note that the Hsia calendar months of Rat (December), Snake (May), and Rooster (September) will be months when allies and friends make the energies favorable. This book contains month to month readings of your luck to highlight the different chi energy of each month. They reveal significant high and low points of each month. The idea is to be alerted auspicious as well as unlucky months.

Nothing works better than to be prepared for sudden reversals of fortune, and in knowing when a particular misfortune can happen. When forewarned you have enough time to put remedies into place and to wear cures to suppress the affliction. This is the best way of avoiding misfortunes! Better to subdue bad luck than to wait for bad things to happen and then regret.

This is what motivates us to carefully research and analyze the Almanacs and source books to bring you accurate monthly readings that are an essential component of these books. Timely warnings are given in the monthly readings on Career, Business, Family, Love and Study luck.

These take into account each month's Lo Shu numbers, element, trigram and paht chee luck pillars. These are usually very accurate not just in identifying your good and bad months, but they also offer valuable advice on when to lie low and when to move confidently forward. It will help you get your timing right on important decisions and actions.

Our books on the 12 animal signs this year follow our tradition of bringing advice that is specific, focused and timely. The recommendations here are meant to alert you to months when you are vulnerable to illness, accidents or dangers. The good luck months are when significant opportunities come to you. Knowing *when* is certain to give you a competitive edge. This year we have added new dimensions that bring yet greater depth to our recommendations on timing.

Your Feng Shui in 2010

A section is devoted to vital Feng Shui updates to be attended to at the start of each New Year. This explains **transformational energy patterns** that create new lucky and unlucky sectors in 2010. You can then make all the necessary adjustments to the feng shui of your home and work place.

Remedial cures are always necessary to dissolve bad energy that brings misfortune, accidents, illness and other afflictions.

All houses are affected by new energy patterns. You may have enjoyed good feng shui last year, but the pattern of chi will have changed in 2010. An excellent example is the NE of the home which is the home location of the Ox. Last year this sector was hit by the harmful quarrelsome star 3 but in 2010, another kind of affliction hits you; this time it's the illness 2. But the good news is that your Ox direction this year enjoys the lucky 24 mountain star of "Big Auspicious" which brings you the success you want!

Element therapy is very effective for neutralizing bad energy patterns such as the illness star and for strengthening the good sectors. This year, the good luck star number 8 is in the center of the chart. This development indicates that the year benefits those whose homes have an open-plan concept that does not 'lock up" this auspicious star.

If you have a toilet or store room in the center of the home, this can cause good luck to dissipate or stagnate; but if the center of your home is an open space, the good fortune chi flows seamlessly into the living areas of the home; and then 8 in the center brings extreme good fortune, more so when you install a bright light here.

When the luck of 8 of the center is able to flow to other sectors, it particularly benefits the SW and NE, as these are locations visited by the afflictive stars 2 and 5, two earth numbers that transform into potential good fortune stars when they connect with the 8 to form the parent string combination of 2/5/8. Such a configuration which suppresses the negative aspect of 2 and 5 is only possible when there are no walls to block the energy of 8 from flowing outwards.

Generating Wealth Luck

This is not going to be an easy year, but there is potential to create wealth. Not the kind of mega quick bucks generated through escalation of capital appreciation; instead, wealth will be made in new areas of creative enterprise. It will also be risky because the Year of the Tiger always holds risks. Riding the Tiger requires courage and nerves of steel!

The world's economy is presently going through a major transformation; we are living through the Age of an Information Revolution where news technology and ideas are accessible to everyone. Wealth comes less from traditional sectors and more from new creativity, technology, energy sources and ways of packaging.

It is advisable to start the Tiger Year by being defensive. You will benefit from being protected so make sure you place cures in all the afflicted sectors of your office and home.

It makes sense to subdue the ferocious side of the Tiger. For those of you with dreams of making money who are also prepared to take the risks, you can symbolically "ride the Tiger" to activate its wealth enhancing potential. But if you are planning on taking business risks this year, you are well advised to enlist the aid of the "Tiger-subduing Deities". Most famous of the Taoist Deities are the Tiger-Taming Lohan, the Wealth God sitting on a Tiger and the Immortal astride the Tiger.

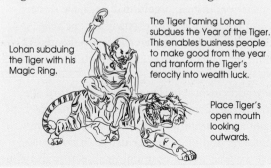

The Tiger Taming Lohan subdues the Year of the Tiger. This enables business people to make good from the year and tranform the Tiger's ferocity into wealth luck.

Lohan subduing the Tiger with his Magic Ring.

Place Tiger's open mouth looking outwards.

Chinese legends contain tales of the wealth-bringing prowess of wise old Tiger, but this can only be unleashed when the wild side of this ferocious beast is adequately tamed! Hence in the Year of the Tiger, it benefits to invite into your home the three powerful deities who control the Tiger. To many Chinese, they are the most powerful of wealth Gods and their presence attracts great wealth.

You can also energize the Earth element for the center of the house to attract wealth. This is because Earth energy stands for wealth luck in 2010. To signify Earth, nothing works better than a **circular orb** rotating in the center of the home to attract wealth luck. So a powerful wealth energizer for the home or any living or work area is to have a **solid rotating crystal ball** in the center. Those that come with an 8 embedded in gold in the center of the crystal ball are the best, although those who believe in the power of mantras can also place the *Om Mani Padme Hum* rotating crystal ball here.

Last year we designed just such a crystal ball. We embossed the 21 Tara Praises onto the ball and these brought so much good fortune for us and to everyone who used them. Rotating the crystal ball makes it very yang and that is what makes it generate fabulous energy. Shine a light onto the crystal to empower it and to make it even more beautiful.

Luck of Elements

Staying lucky requires you to be personally empowered. The aura around you must be radiant and strong, not stagnant and weary. Hence being properly energized, healthy and staying astrologically strong are the three ingredients of attaining success luck in any year.

What is important is to know exactly how your own personal elements interact with the elements of the year in 5 important categories. Each of you, depending on your year of birth, are born with different elements that affect the strength and quality of your **Life Force**; your **Inner Essence**; your **Success Potential**, the stability of your **Financial Luck** and the state of your **Health Luck**.

Your horoscope reveals the ruling elements that govern each of the 5 categories of luck, and how they interact with the 5 luck elements of the year. In 2010, the Life Force of the year is Wood, and its Spirit Essence is Water. Hence you can see that it is Water that strengthens Wood… it is the *Spirit Essence* that strengthens the *Life Force* of the year.

The year's *Health Luck* is governed also by Wood while both the year's *financial* and *success* potential are governed by Metal. To find out how each person's birth elements interact with the luck elements of the year, we need to analyze how each person's elements interact with 2010's elements. This provides important information that enables you to enhance your potential enormously.

The analysis is based on your year of birth, your heavenly stem and your earthly branch. Once you know how strong or how weak your horoscope elements are in 2010, you can easily dress, live and arrange your living space accordingly. This is discussed in detail for you in Part One of this book.

Power of Talismans

Protective talismans have the power to ward off misfortunes and each New Year, it is incredibly important to know what talismans to wear and place in your home to ward off bad luck. In the Tiger Year, the imbalance of energy must be attended to if you want the year to be smooth for you. Protective amulets possess added potency when made correctly. Usually, circular discs and squares make excellent shapes for amulets. The built-in Metal element energy of amulets made of steel or brass with gold finish have great power to suppress illness and misfortune brought by the year's afflictive star energies.

The Chinese Almanac is an excellent source of talisman designs and good Almanacs provide detailed images with invocations and explanations. These are older, rare editions which we have compiled over the years as reference materials to ensure the amulets made comply with vital specifications.

We have discovered that Tibetan style talismans are very potent; these incorporate Sanskrit and Tibetan mantras which are really extremely powerful. In the old days, Tibetan protection amulets were created by monasteries or very high lamas. These usually comprised mantras and images written onto paper and then folded to resemble mystical knots. Traditional talismans are often covered by 5 colored cloth and tied with 5 colored string which signify the 5 elements. Modern day amulets maintain the essence of the talismans but their quality of production is much better. In terms of potency they are equally powerful, if not more so, as modern technology has made it possible to have incredible number of mantras to be inserted into the amulets!

Tiger Year Talismans

Here are some important amulets and rituals required for the coming year.

Double 6 Big Smooth Coins

This is a powerful enhancing good luck charm suitable for this year as it invokes the *Star of Powerful Mentors*. The six large coins made of metal with gold finish ensure everything goes smoothly for you. Having it in your possession will bring you influential help of someone powerful when you need it. Those in leadership or managerial positions will benefit from this coins. Ox people wanting to get ahead up the career ladder should invest in this amulet.

The Tai Sui Amulet

This will invoke the protection and goodwill of the Tai Sui who this year is once again a military general. This amulet carries a special Taoist invocation and the image of a pair of Pi Yao. The Ox born is not directly affected by the Tai Sui but being so near to the Tiger in the compass location it is a good idea to carry the amulet anyway.

Tai Sui Amulet.

The Double Circle Amulet

This is to ward off seriously troublesome chi brought by the combination of the Five Yellow with the illness star affliction. Wearing it as a pendant or hanging it in your animal sign direction is an effective way of overcoming the troublesome months where the configuration of star numbers brings combined danger of illness and misfortune.

The Magic Fire Wheel Talisman

This is the Dharmachakra eight-spoked wheel surrounded by a circle of fire, indicating fire and gold energy. Inscribed in the circle is a very powerful mantra for subduing quarrelsome energy directed towards you. This talisman can effectively reduce gossip, slander, and office politics and even help you avoid court cases and legal entanglements. If you can consecrate these magic fire wheels, they are also effective protection against spirit harm.

Magic Fire
Wheel Talisman.

5 Element Ringing Bell

The sound of metal hitting against metal creates the chi energy that can dissolve the power of the Five Yellow which in 2010 hurts the matriarch in all families. It is important not only to have this bell displayed in the SW corners of the home, but ringing the bell at least once a week magnifies its strength many times over. Walk round each of your rooms in an anti clockwise direction three times, all the while ringing the bell. This is an energy cleansing ritual which is safe and effective to use. It was not easy finding the kind of bell that produces the melodious sounds preferred for these bell amulets. But when you ring the bell, you are instantly dissolving bad energy built up in your space. Do this ritual in rooms that are important to you. Ox born people should undertake the bell ringing ritual on Thursdays of the week.

Excellent for NW & West and absolutely essential in the SW. This is an excellent cure for overcoming the *wu wang*, which in 2010 hurts the matriarch. Mantras embossed on the bell empowers it.

5-ELEMENT
RINGING BELL

Blue Water in a Globe

This *water* element talisman is a potent way of making up for the lack of water this year. Carrying the Water in a Globe Amulet everywhere you go symbolically brings growth luck. Water feeds the wood energy of the year and this amulet is especially suitable for those born in the year of the Ox. Having it is sure to add strength to your life force making it easier for good fortune to manifest for you during the year.

A drop of water is like an ocean. The Water element brings prosperity in 2010.

Good Income Luck Talisman

Fashioned as a wealth vase, this amulet contains the Taoist wealth fu written on one side and coins and ingots on the other side. The good income luck talisman is excellent to wear to protect against being laid off, losing one's source of income or to ensure that good business luck continues.

Precious Ring Talisman

This powerful Ring talisman is said to possess magical powers. It is the main tool of the Tiger-Taming Arhat who was a Brahmin named Pindola. Made of steel and plated with real gold, inside the ring can be inserted powerful Dharmakaya mantras. The ring can be hung in the NE of your living room or office, or you can carry it with you as a bag hanging. The precious ring talisman is one of the most powerful ways of subduing the negative energies of a Tiger Year.

Precious Ring Talisman for taming the Tiger in 2010. The ring is hollow inside, so precious Dharmakaya mantras can be inserted.

Part 1
Outlook for
the Year 2010

- Fire Ox – 13 & 73 years
- Earth Ox – 61 years
- Metal Ox – 49 years
- Water Ox – 37 years
- Wood Ox – 25 years

The Ox goes into 2010 with the *Star of Big Auspicious* bringing a very special kind of good fortune, but handicapped in its quest for perfection by the illness star. This can slow down the Ox, who has weak energy this year. The Ox is also affected by the Tai Sui occupying the sector next to it. Despite these indications of aggravations to its health, all 5 types of Ox (categorised according to their years of birth and hence the element of their heavenly stem) enjoy superlative luck in attaining success in their professional life or in making superb gains in their net worth.

Of the 5 types of Ox, it is the Water Ox that enjoys the most superlative luck of both Finance and Success. The only thing standing in the way of some major success for the Ox this year is the danger to its health, indicated by the illness star affliction as well as the low level of its life force chi. As long as the correct remedies are installed and worn on the body, nothing should hold the Ox back from attaining great success this year.

The Ox Personality in 2010

The Ox is known as one of the most hardworking of the 12 Zodiac animal signs. They are also tough and resilient, and have an incredible ability to stay focused on their aspirations and ambitions. As such, in anything they do, they are always in for the long term. Their fortitude and courage eventually lands them the winning hand, because in the end, they almost always succeed and get their way. This is due as much to their own tireless efforts as to the strength of their personal convictions.

In 2010, the Ox continues to chase the dream and to build on its vision. This is a year when despite low chi energy, they continue to have the ability to achieve much. This does not mean their confidence level is high. Far from it, the Ox suffers from pangs of insecurity, although no one would guess looking at their outward show of self assurance. Whatever doubts the Ox has are always kept closely hidden – this is their style and their nature. Most times when they come across stubborn, dogmatic or impatient, it is only a manifestation of their own doubts surfacing inside themselves. This is the situation for most of the time in 2010.

As an Ox person, you need to reassure yourself that no one expects you to be perfect. You may not realize it, but many people admire you for your vision, your ideals and your tenacity in the face of the risks that you take. Thus while 2010 could during some months appear to be giving you a hard time, it benefits for you to bite back the urge to throw in the towel. But hang in there because success and financial luck is not bad at all. Remember you are blessed with the sign of Big Auspicious!

It also benefits for you to develop some patience this year. Make an effort to loosen up. Laugh. Have a sense of humor. And should there be any remote reason at all to go take a medical check up, do so. Please try not to be stubborn about these things; with the illness star hovering threateningly in your sign, there is real danger that you might succumb to some disease or sudden illness. Stay healthy and keep an eye out for whatever risks may be out there.

LADY OX

Birth Year	Type of Ox Lady	Lo Shu at Birth	Age	Luck Outlook in 2010
1937	Fire Ox Lady	9	73	No worries on the money side
1949	Earth Ox Lady	6	61	This lady holds a winning hand
1961	Metal Ox Lady	3	49	Success luck but not much else
1973	Water Ox Lady	9	37	Excellent success & money luck
1985	Wood Ox Lady	6	25	Professionally on a roll
1997	Fire Ox Lady	3	13	Outlook for success is good

The Lady Ox will discover who her real friends are in 2010. This is a year when she has much on her plate and there are occasions when she will need to call on friends for assistance. There will be moments through the year when she discovers that she may have bitten off more than she can chew, and this fills her with self doubt.

When she needs help however, her friends are too busy with problems of their own. The Ox lady does not enjoy the luck of having friends leap to her side this year; but despite a full work schedule, the Ox lady has some formidable organisational skills of management – the home kind as well as the office variety, so that in the end, she copes most efficiently. She is after all an excellent administrator, capable of wearing different hats at the same time.

Professionally, the lady Ox tends to fare better than the men this year simply because women tend to be more patient and this is a year when patience is a key quality to have. There are many moments when your aggravation level will reach breaking point, but staying cool and calm helps you beat the blues!

Carry the blue rhino and elephant hanging for protection against burglary and snatch thieves.

The female of the Ox sign will be engulfed with many moments of self doubt but will be strong enough to brush these aside in the interest of keeping her head above water. She is not terribly strong in 2010 and her resistance to illness is also at a low ebb. More alarming is that her chi strength is low and this can be a cause for concern. All Ox women need to stay strong, have enough sleep and the younger ones among you should watch you don't, make sure not to party too hard. There are hidden dangers in staying out too late at nights. Exercise caution when out by yourself!

The Lady Ox should wear the heart sutra scarf at all times especially when out late at nights. This will protect against hidden & unexpected dangers in the Year of the Tiger.

GENTLEMAN OX

Birth Year	Type of Ox Man	Lo Shu at Birth	Age	Luck Outlook in 2010
1937	Fire Ox Man	9	73	Good financial & success luck
1949	Earth Ox Man	6	61	Staying grounded brings success
1961	Metal Ox Man	3	49	Professionally a successful year
1973	Water Ox Man	9	37	Enormous Success Luck
1985	Wood Ox Man	6	25	Work wise a great year for you
1997	Fire Ox Man	3	13	A good year for you

The Gentleman Ox stays resolutely focused on work and getting ahead this year, especially the younger Wood and Water Ox gentlemen. As a result, they tend to overwork and this route is not at all good for you. You must not forget you are at risk of falling critically ill this year as you are afflicted by the illness star.

Every Ox suffers from a low life force and there is a double negative against your chi strength. Hence the advice is for you to take things easy and not be too uptight about work or business. In terms of success and financial gains, most of you have a good store of this kind of luck. So worrying is unnecessary. Mentally, the Ox guy finds it hard to let go of responsibilities and work-related issues. You really are the ultimate workaholic, so full of good intentions and finding it so hard to lighten up and let go.

The Water Ox guy enjoys superlative finance and success luck and the youngster of 13 years will discover big moments of triumph this year.

Ox men are clever individuals, often brilliant at what they do and able to spot good opportunities. This is how they rise to positions of leadership. This year sees them enjoy material success luck, so we are likely to see them at their best. However, ill health can slow them down, so there is a need to be mindful in looking after themselves physically.

Getting sick can be a very annoying development in anyone's life, but you, the Ox will feel it more acutely. So it is definitely worthwhile to look after your health and also to wear feng shui amulets that protect you.

The Ox male may face health issues this year, hence should carry the wu lou as a personal amulet to negate this kind of bad luck.

Personal Luck Horoscope in 2010

This section focuses on the Personal Luck Horoscope of the Ox in 2010. The horoscope chart of elements for each Ox person is determined by the *heavenly stem* element of your year of birth.

The Horoscope Chart shows how the Ox's ruling luck elements in its year of birth interacts with the luck elements of the year 2010. This interaction reveals 5 important kinds of good luck and the Horoscope reveals whether these 5 types of luck is good or bad each year.

When the elements governing the 5 kinds of luck for each animal sign (using its year of birth) interact with the 2010 elements governing the same kinds of luck, this interaction reveals whether the year brings strength or weakness to that type of luck. It is extremely beneficial to examine what kind of luck combination your animal sign's element horoscope brings each year as these change from year to year. Let's look at these 5 types of luck:

First, Your Life Force...

This reveals hidden dangers or threats to your life that can cause premature death or bring severe worries. This can come suddenly, with little warning, and death can also come to perfectly healthy people through accidents or unexpected natural disaster. In recent years, raging wild fires, widespread floods, earthquakes and other natural disasters have brought havoc suddenly and unexpectedly into people's lives. So looking out for such threats is an important aspect of horoscope consultations.

When the Life Force luck shows a double cross – XX – it is vital to wear some kind of **celestial amulet**. The best form of protection is usually something spiritual, a set of sacred syllables or a talisman that carries powerful holy mantras.

A double XX does not necessarily bring death. What it brings is a warning that some kind of danger is imminent. Usually, if the wearing of amulets is accompanied by some good deed such as performing *animal liberation* or *donating to some charity*, danger is successfully averted. Threats to the Life Force are usually karmic and these can be assuaged by a specific kind action on your part.

A circle and a cross – OX or XO – suggests you need some kind of protection because there is a likelihood of some small accident or event happening that could cause a great deal of inconvenience and aggravation. Those whose Life Force shows a single X must watch what they eat. You must be mindful of your speech also, because what you say can bring an unexpected negative reaction.

Be mindful of your interactive behaviour with others. Guard against arrogance and if you should get into a fight or argument, it is advisable to walk away. Give the victory to those who annoy you! Hard to do, but very beneficial if your Life Force is showing either one or two Xs. This will dissipate any bad luck you may be experiencing.

When a double or triple O such as OO or OOO your Life Force enjoys, it means you will be very strong and no harm threatens you during the year. Anyone attempting to cause you hurt will find it all rebounds back to them!

> For those with a Life Force indication of OO or OOO, it will be impossible for anyone with bad intentions to harm you, as you are under powerful cosmic protection. The Chinese respect this energy and refer to it as a magical aura of protection. It is like a guardian angel watching over you.

Second, Your Health Luck...

This is a direct barometer of your physical health. If yours is showing a double cross - XX - it means that 2010 could bring vulnerability to health issues. When health luck is not good, work schedules and grand plans get blocked. Poor health luck means you can get food poisoning easily, and you can catch wind born diseases. Even a single cross - X - suggests some kind of health-related aggravation.

It is believed that bad health luck is brought by the winds. So an excellent way of overcoming the double or single X in your Health Luck is to hang a **wu lou** to appease the winds in your animal sign location.

In 2010, the Ox is afflicted by being indirectly hit by the Tai Sui, so this might add to the bad health luck of the 49 year old Ox and the 37 year old Ox. So for both of you, it benefits to place a **Metal Wu Lou** or the **Antahkarana Symbol** nearby as a remedy.

The double circle - OO – against your Health Luck suggests there are no health aggravations at all for you. Those who were sick last year will get better. Good health indications suggest a happy state of mind with no mental aggravations. You have an excellent positive attitude which attracts good fortune. A single circle – O – also signals a welcoming attitude. So the 61 year old Ox is probably the happiest of all the Ox this year.

Those whose charts indicate a cross and a circle – XO or OX – have little cause to worry because the circle overrides the cross, so the year will flow smoothly unless your animal sign is hit by the illness star affliction.

Third, Your Finance Luck...

This part of the Horoscope reveals the strength and stability of your economic situation. It also indicates if you can improve your financial situation during the year i.e. whether you can do better than the previous year.

When a double circle – OO – is placed against this type of luck in your chart, it means you can gain substantial new wealth in 2010, and when your chart indicates three circles – OOO – it means your wealth luck is even more certain to materialise! Your business will prosper and whatever expansion you are planning is sure to bear fruit. This is the case with the 37 year old Water Ox. Remember we have said that Water is the element that is most lacking in 2010, so the double Water element of this Ox's heavenly stem brings it prosperity luck.

A single circle - O - means the year does not bring much change to your finances and you will enjoy a stable situation. There will be few surprises to make you worry.

An indication of crosses is a negative reading. The more crosses there are, the greater the instability of your financial situation. The double cross - XX - indicates ups and downs in your money luck.

Business suddenly takes a downturn and profits get hit by declines. Bad financial luck indications must be countered; and you can do this by making some kind of charitable contribution to ease somebody's financial burden. Generosity is the best antidote to lack of financial good fortune.

Buddhists recommend making offerings to the **White Dzambhala Wealth Deity** who sits on a Dragon, carries the gem spouting mongoose and is attended to by four offering goddesses. This is a powerful antidote to counter unstable money luck. If you even have a single cross - X - against your Finance Luck, you should avoid starting any new business ventures or making investments in property or dabble too much in the stock market. You should be extra careful with your funds. Be conservative. A cross with a circle - OX or XO - indicates a stable situation that is neither very bad nor very good.

Fourth, Your Success Luck...

This category puts attention on how well you will do in your career for the year. It offers accurate indications about prospects for promotion and also tracks your progress at work, in school or in anything that you may be engaged in doing at the moment. It also affects those involved in a competitive situation. The circles and crosses are a measure of how successful you can be.

When three circles – OOO – or two circles – OO – appear, it indicates wonderful recognition and success in all your endeavors; your career, work, exams or performance in any competition. When you have three circles, you attain recognition easily as the year's energies favor you. All those born in years of the Ox benefit from having OOO against their Success Luck. The Ox also enjoys the *Star of Big Auspicious* brought by the 24 Mountains. Hence in terms of success, the Ox is described as enjoying excellent luck indeed!

Two circles means success with some effort. A single circle – O – is a positive indication of success, but you need to refrain from getting big headed. A circle with a cross – OX or XO – suggests support from your direct supervisor or boss but you may not have the support of colleagues and co-workers. Make sure you watch your feng shui at work and do not sit with your back to the door.

When two crosses – XX - appear, they indicate aggravations at work and obstacles that block your success. There will be unexpected setbacks and unhelpful people who bring out the worst in you, making you stumble and falter. None of you born in Ox years however suffers from this affliction in 2010.

Fifth, Your Spirit Essence...

This last category is in many ways the most important as it reveals insights into your inner resilience and spiritual strength. When the inner essence of your persona is resistant to spiritual afflictions, you can more easily overcome the lack of other categories of luck.

When it is weak, it makes you vulnerable to the negative effect of various *wandering spirits*. While many of these local spirits are harmless, there are some who can be harmful if you inadvertently anger them; through saying wrong things that get picked up by the winds, by desecrating their "homes" such as cutting down old trees or digging up ant hills without ritually seeking permission to do so. These worldly ghosts can only harm those with low levels of spirit essence indicated by the crosses. But anyone getting hit by them will get sick and doctors cannot find the cause, yet you can get weaker and weaker. This is the most obvious way of knowing you have been afflicted.

A very low spirit essence is indicated by two crosses – XX – although when you get even a single X, you are advised to protect yourself with powerful mantra amulets. Wearing anything with mantras or sutras inscribed on them is very beneficial as this will ensures that your excellent Success Luck is adequately protected against spirit harm.

Sometimes people who dislike you for whatever reason can also use black magic against you. Again, these are usually effective only when your Spirit Essence is low. The best protection is to wear protective mantras on your body such as a mantra ring or a seed syllable such as *Hum* or *Om*. These offer powerful protection. You can also wear mantra pendants and necklaces in gold, or the powerful protective **Kalachakra Pendant**.

When you encounter a cross and a circle – XO or OX – this suggests anger but also indicates that you will be shielded from any severe effect.

Circles means you have inbuilt protection against spiritual afflictions. A single circle – O – indicates you are blessed and protected from spirit harm. A double or triple circle – OOO - means that there are guardian Buddhas, angels or dakinis (holy beings) watching over you. This is a very lucky and auspicious meaning as it reflects that you are fully protected during the year. You are not just spiritually safe but will also be shielded against poor health, loss of wealth and obstacles that spoil your success luck.

PERSONAL LUCK
13 & 73 Year Old Fire Ox

Type of Luck	Element at Birth affecting this Luck	Element in 2010 affecting this Luck	Luck Rating
Life Force	Earth	Wood	XX
Health Luck	Water	Wood	OX
Finance Luck	Fire	Metal	OO
Success Luck	Water	Metal	OOO
Spirit Essence	Fire	Water	XX

The Fire Ox's Element Horoscope Chart shown above indicates excellent Success Luck and very good financial luck. However, Health Luck is average and both the life force and chi strength registers a double negative. This means you are psychically weak this year and you need to make sure your negatives are subdued.

The 73 year old should watch for health issues while the 13 year old Fire Ox is too young to be affected by the double X ratings in the Life Force and Chi Strength. It can be interpreted that while the illness affliction is dangerous for older Ox, it is less so for the young teenager Ox.

Average Health Luck is indicated, which reassures the Fire Ox somewhat. This is a positive indication for the older Fire Ox. It means that in 2010 there won't be too many troublesome health issues. There are also no major setbacks for you and the economic situation looks stable.

What might be a troubling to the Fire Ox is the double cross - XX- that points to some negativity in Spiritual Essence. This can be regarded as its Chi Strength for the year and a double negative indicates negativity of some kind. This sign of potential danger can be overcome by wearing an amulet or some kind of protection. The double cross here is a warning to be careful when out and about. Try not to stay out too late as the yin hours of the night pose some real dangers.

Wear or carry mantra amulets which will afford you good protection and guidance. If you can, carry the **Heart Sutra Scarf** with you at all times. It is light and small, so it is very portable, but it is extremely powerful; perfect for overcoming your double negative.

61 Year Old Earth Ox

Type of Luck	Element at Birth affecting this Luck	Element in 2010 affecting this Luck	Luck Rating
Life Force	Earth	Wood	XX
Health Luck	Fire	Wood	OOO
Finance Luck	Earth	Metal	OX
Success Luck	Water	Metal	OOO
Spirit Essence	Fire	Water	XX

The Earth Ox enjoys superb health and success luck in 2010, supposedly the best as the indication is a maximum three circles. These are very good indications that for 61 year old Earth Ox, despite the year being rather unstable and lacking in good news, for this Ox, the world can pass by without affecting you in any negative way. Financially it is not a great indication, but it is also not bad.

The Ox ruled by the Earth Element may not have the same kind of imagination as the other Ox types but this is only because the Earth element ensures it stays practical and down to earth with realistic expectations on what life has to offer. In any situation, this is a very highly responsible Ox who can be depended on. There is a sincerity about the way he/she responds to friends and colleagues.

The year can be said to bring some good luck for this Ox who has just retired or is about to do so. You have material and financial stability. These are down to earth matters important to the Ox, so looking at the year from this perspective, it is likely to satisfy this Ox despite its Life Force and Chi Strength being low.

Nevertheless, the double cross is cause for concern as it indicates a vulnerability of some kind of problem caused by either Spirit Harm or due to some health issue. This strongly suggests that the Ox should play safe and get some spiritual protective remedies.

49 Year Old Metal Ox

Type of Luck	Element at Birth affecting this Luck	Element in 2010 affecting this Luck	Luck Rating
Life Force	Earth	Wood	XX
Health Luck	Earth	Wood	XX
Finance Luck	Metal	Metal	X
Success Luck	Water	Metal	OOO
Spirit Essence	Fire	Water	XX

The Metal Ox is perhaps the least lucky of all Ox this year although it does have excellent Success Luck. This is a very good indication that good fortune does not desert you completely during the year and you can continue to make your mark professionally or in business. The Success Luck shown here is at maximum levels and this indicates some kind of impressive outcome for you in the achievement area.

However, all other indicated luck types show a negative cross and as for the health indications, which includes your life force, these indicate that you might well be in a precarious situation. Viewed in the context of your affliction to the illness star in the feng shui chart of the year, the two crosses in your health luck is a definite cause for concern. This added to the double cross of your Life Force is ringing some bells in the head. You should take these signs seriously. You must make a real effort to wear protective mantras and especially the special **Antahkarana Ring** as this will give you powerful protection against falling sick.

The Metal Ox is probably the most vocal and combative of all the Ox types and also the most authoritative – however, in 2010, very little of this side of you is on show. In 2010 you are neither intimidating nor unbending, and this comes as a surprise close to you. The Metal Ox is usually a strong personality who rarely if ever presents a weak side. In 2010 however, although you are still relatively young, you find yourself being weak mentally and physically. As such, you might become uncharacteristically sentimental and even allow yourself to get emotional. Your public persona is also weak this year. Some of the spark seems to have deserted you.

The Metal Ox should wear the Antahkarana Ring to give powerful protection against falling sick.

37 Year Old Water Ox

Type of Luck	Element at Birth affecting this Luck	Element in 2010 affecting this Luck	Luck Rating
Life Force	Earth	Wood	XX
Health Luck	Wood	Wood	X
Finance Luck	Water	Metal	OOO
Success Luck	Water	Metal	OOO
Spirit Essence	Fire	Water	XX

The Water Ox has absolutely superb Financial and Success Luck – three circles – which show that in terms of attaining business or money goals, you will definitely do better than you expect. In fact in 2010, the Water element is in such short supply that anyone with the element of Water in their horoscope is sure to enjoy some good money luck! This is true of all twelve signs of the Zodiac.

In terms of ambitions, the Water Ox is indeed unrelentingly ambitious, although this does not make it a tense workaholic. Surprisingly, this most ambitious of Ox is also the most relaxed when interacting with others.

Since your money luck is good this year, the pressure of the previous year should have eased. Nevertheless, do continue to have your water feature in the SE of your house and invite Lord Dzambhala, the Buddha of Wealth into your home, then perform the daily 7 water bowl offerings ritual to request continued financial stability. We recommend the water feature because this year is going to be a very thirsty year that is totally lacking in water. This comes from a reading of the paht chee chart of the year. As such, anyone with water will have an edge over those who do not.

The worrisome indication for 2010 concerns everyone born in ann Ox year. The illness 2 brings serious illness issues making the Ox vulnerable. This is made worse by the double cross against your Life Force and Spirit Essence. So it is quite likely that yin spirit forces might disturb you. Hang the **Mantra Protection Plaque** in the NE above entrances and wear personal mantra rings, bracelets or pendants to ensure protection. Christians can wear the crucifix for protection.

25 Year Old Wood Ox

Type of Luck	Element at Birth affecting this Luck	Element in 2010 affecting this Luck	Luck Rating
Life Force	Earth	Wood	XX
Health Luck	Metal	Wood	00
Finance Luck	Wood	Metal	XX
Success Luck	Water	Metal	000
Spirit Essence	Fire	Water	XX

The 25 year old Wood Ox goes into 2010 still on a high, as its working life and career continue to hum along. There is excellent success luck for you this year. You may be in line for some upward mobility in terms of having extra responsibilities heaped on you. Should this happen and you find you are being asked to do the job of three people, accept the challenge! Work never killed anyone, least of all a strong Ox like you!

In 2010 your Life Force may be weak, but your Health Luck is good, and this means you can make your body and mind healthy and tough. It is all up to you so make up your mind to stay healthy and beat the illness affliction that is afflicting you in 2010. The best way is to take up some healthy sport. Note that staying healthy is breathing in the fresh air, not merely working out at the gym. Staying in shape is not necessarily staying healthy.

Financially, it is not a great year; but remember you are still very young and at this age, it is far better to gain experience and have opportunities come to you than to have too much money. With prosperity always comes responsibilities and it is definitely better to wait a little for the money luck to come. As long as opportunities open up for you and you continue to excel at your job, you are doing very well!

Watch you do not allow excessive idealism make life overly complicated for you.

The Wood Ox has a worldview that embraces integrity and ethics so an underlying streak of conservatism influences the way you work and respond. But you are also very pragmatic and this brings wonderful potential for success.

Part 2
Ox Relationships

In Chinese Astrology, your animal sign creates a variety of influences on your life, most significant of which is how it affects the way you interact with the people around you, your partner, your parents, children, siblings, relatives & friends.

Knowing the fundamentals of astrological compatibilities can help you make your relationships more harmonious, uplifting and definitely less aggravating. You will understand your reactions to people, why you have a natural affinity with some and an instant aversion to others; why some people just annoy you for no reason and why you easily overlook the faults of some others.

It all boils down to the affinity groupings, the secret friends and ideal soul mate pairings of the Chinese Zodiac! The Horoscope compatibility groupings influence how you respond to each of the other eleven signs and explain the special relationships that inherently exist between them.

However, there are annual variations to the level of compatibility amongst animal signs. Everyone's energies, moods, aspirations and tolerance levels change from year to year. People tend to be more or less tolerant, more or less magnanimous or selfish, more distracted or warm depending on how they fare during any year.

When things go smoothly one is better disposed to others and even between two animal signs who are naturally antagonistic, there can still be good affinity, enough for two unlikely animal signs to enjoy one another to the extent of becoming temporary soul mates!

Likewise when one is being challenged by a non-stop set of problems, then the slightest provocation can lead to anger even between zodiac friends and allies. That is when friends can become temporary enemies! A falling out between horoscope allies is not impossible.

Hence compatibility between animal signs takes account of time frames.

In this section, we look at how the Ox person interacts with the other animal signs in detail.

Compatibility Groupings

1. Alliance of Allies
2. Paired Soulmates
3. Secret Friends
4. Astrological Enemies
5. Peach Blossom Links
6. Seasonal Trinity

1. Alliance of Allies

There are four affinity groupings of animal signs that make up Alliances of Allies. Each Alliance comprises three animal signs that are natural allies of the Horoscope. The three signs within any Alliance have similar outlooks and share similar goals. Their attitudes and thought processes are alike, and their support of and compatibility with each other tends to be instant and natural.

When all three animal signs enjoy good fortune in any year, the Alliance becomes strong and powerful that year. When there is a natural Alliance within a family unit as amongst siblings, or between spouses and a child, the family tends to be very united. They give strength to one another, and when they prosper, good fortune gets multiplied. Families that have Alliances of Allies are usually extremely close knit. This is one of the secret indications of good fortune. As an Alliance, they become a formidable force.

Allies always get along. Any falling out is temporary. They trust and depend on each other and immediately close ranks should there be an external threat. Good personal feng shui comes from carrying the symbolic image of your Horoscope Allies, especially when they are going through good years.

Ally Groupings	Animals	Characteristics
Competitors	Rat, Dragon, Monkey	Competent, Tough, Resolute
Intellectuals	Ox, Snake, Rooster	Generous, Focused, Resilient
Enthusiastic	Dog, Tiger, Horse	Aggressive, Rebellious, Coy
Diplomatic	Boar, Sheep, Rabbit	Creative, Kind, Emotional

The Ox and its Allies are advised to stay close in 2010 as their Lo Shu numbers in the year's chart create the sum of ten. This brings powerful prosperity opportunities to them as a group. This Alliance enjoys special energy this year so if they work and do business as a team, collectively putting up a strong front, they are certain to benefit. If your business associates and you comprise this grouping of Ox, Snake and Rooster, the year holds some genuinely exciting opportunities.

In the Alliance, the Ox is advised to give way to the Snake or Rooster's leadership, as the Ox is in the weakest position. Your luck is great this year apart from illness threats. But your Life Force and Chi Energy are at a low ebb and this does make a difference to the way luck manifests for you. You need the strength of your Allies, the Snake and the Rooster. If there are three of you in a family, or within the same department of a company, the Alliance can be activated to benefit every member.

Of the three, it is you, the Ox whose chi is the weakest and Snake whose chi is strongest. The Ox has a negative rating in the Life Force and Inner Strength stakes. So it benefits the Ox to carry images of the Snake and Rooster to ensure you go through the year smoothly. This will help you to actualize the Alliance of Allies, helping your own financial and success luck to actualize. The Ox will suffer from bouts of depression and insecurity. There could be moments when your normal high confidence deserts you. But your instincts are good and you must continue to rely on your own judgement. But in this Alliance, do give way and let others take the lead.

2. Paired Soulmates

There are six pairs of animal signs that can be described as natural soul mates. One sign will be yin and the other yang. In astrology texts they are described as creating the six **Zodiac Houses** with each one manifesting its own special niche of compatibility. The pairing creates a powerful bonding on a cosmic level, and a marriage or business union between any two people belonging to the same Zodiac House will have instant rapport with each other.

When people talk about 'falling in love at first sight' it is likely they belong to the same House; and should they marry, there is promise of great happiness for them. The Soulmates pairing spells happiness more than any other kind of Zodiac alliance. This combination also works well professionally – e.g. as professional partners in a practice - and between siblings, brothers or sisters. The mutual strength of each pair is different, as some make better commercial partners than marriage partners. How successful you are as a pair depends on how deeply you bond and also whether you have serious interests in common.

Houses of Paired Soulmates

Animals	Yin/ Yang	Zodiac House of Creativity	Target Unleashed
Rat	Yang	House of Creativity & Cleverness	The Rat initiates
Ox	Yin		The Ox completes
Tiger	Yang	House of Growth & Development	The Tiger employs force
Rabbit	Yin		The Rabbit uses diplomacy
Dragon	Yang	House of Magic & Spritituality	The Dragon creates magic
Snake	Yin		The Snake creates mystery
Horse	Yang	House of Passion & Sexuality	The Horse embodies male energy
Sheep	Yin		The Sheep is the female energy
Monkey	Yang	House of Career & Commerce	The Monkey creates strategy
Rooster	Yin		The Rooster get things moving
Dog	Yang	House of Domesticity	The Dog works to provide
Boar	Yin		The Boar enjoys what is created

A coming together of the yin Ox with its soulmate the yang Rat creates the **House of Creativity and Cleverness**; This is a strong alliance because these two are also secret friends, so whenever they get together, there is already a powerful bond underlying their friendship. In 2010, neither have very strong Life Force luck, but the Rat is stronger.

Rat's energy levels can be described as average, but Ox is weak. Should they get together in a business arrangement, it will benefit greatly from the creativity and clever inputs they both bring to the venture. Here they inspire one another. The partnership will succeed whether on a professional or personal level; how successful depends on the luck of the year, and 2010 brings luck that is just average. But the ingenuity of this pair will surface and work to their advantage. Here Rat initiates and Ox brings things to completion, mainly because Ox is more disciplined and serious about work than Rat.

The Rat is in danger of getting distracted; nevertheless an alliance between this pair is mutually beneficial. The Ox also brings the 24 Mountain Star of Big Auspicious to the pairing. They should thus do well as business partners.

3. Secret Friends

There is a third set of very special relationships in the Zodiac groupings, and this creates a secret friendship where a powerful affinity exists. This makes them exceptionally compatible. This is a vigorous union of two equals and works best as a married couple. There is love, respect and goodwill between secret friends. Theirs is a bond, which once forged will be hard to break; and even when they themselves want to break it will be hard for either party to fully walk away.

Pairings of Secret Friends

Rat	Boar	Dog	Dragon	Snake	Horse
Ox	Tiger	Rabbit	Rooster	Monkey	Sheep

This pair of signs will stick together through thick and thin. They are fiercely protective of each other and even when they are not partners there is still some kind of instant comradeship and simpatico between them. But one will dominate and it is usually the animal sign whose heavenly stem element controls the other. In the pairing of secret friends, the Ox is paired with the Rat and hence there is a very special bond between these two animal signs as they are also Soulmates of the Zodiac.

4. Astrological Enemies

According to the principles of the Horoscope, the animal sign that directly confronts yours is your astrological enemy who can never help you. For the Ox, the enemy is the Sheep. Note that your enemy does not necessarily harm you; it only means someone of this sign can never be of any real help to you. The elements of the two of you are Yin Earth so you are definitely extremely competitive with each other.

There is a six year gap between the two signs and any pairing between them is unlikely to benefit either side. They cannot have sincere intentions towards one another. Marriage between an Ox and a Sheep is unlikely to bring lasting happiness unless there are other indications in their respective paht chee charts. Pairings between arrows of antagonism are usually discouraged by those who investigate Zodiac compatibilities.

Pairings of Astrological Enemies

Rat	Boar	Dog	Rabbit	Tiger	Ox
Horse	Snake	Dragon	Rooster	Monkey	Sheep

Ox are advised to refrain from getting involved with a Sheep. As a business partnership, the pairing is likely to lead to problems, and in the event of a split, the separation can be acrimonious even if they start out as best friends. In 2010 any coming together of the Ox and Sheep will be full of obstacles. Both signs have afflictions and their latent hostility could well make them intolerant of each other. Better not to take this relationship too far as you will only feel sorry later on.

When two opposite signs have a hostile connection this way and they stay in the same house, they cannot be close; they have a completely different sets of friends. If they are siblings they will not share confidences and will eventually drift apart. If they stay apart, there will not be any direct antagonism, but they are unlikely to have much in common.

5. Peach Blossom Links

Each of the Alliance of Allies has a special relationship with one of the four primary signs of Horse, Rat, Rooster and Rabbit in that these are the symbolic representations of love and romance for one alliance group of animal signs. In the Horoscope, they are referred to as *peach blossom animals* and the presence of their images in the homes of the matching alliance of allies brings peach blossom luck, which is associated with love and romance.

The Ox belongs to the Alliance of Snake, Rooster and Ox, and they have the Horse as their peach blossom link. The Ox will benefit from associating with anyone born in the Horse year, and will also benefit from placing a painting or image of a Horse in the South corner of the house, or in the Ox direction of NE.

6. Seasonal Trinity

There is another grouping of animal signs which create the four seasonal trinity combinations that bring exceptional luck of seasonal abundance. To many astrology experts this is regarded as one of the more powerful combinations of animal signs. When the combination exists within a family made up of either parent or both parents with one or more children, they will collectively be strong enough to transform the luck indications for the family for the entire year.

This means that even when annual indications may not appear favorable, the existence of the seasonal combination of animals within any living abode is sufficient to transform the luck, making it a lot better. The best times will also always be felt by the season indicated by the combination.

It is however necessary for all three animal signs to live together or be in the same office working in close proximity for this powerful pattern to take effect.

Seasonal Trinities of the Horoscope

Animal signs	Season	Element	Direction
Dragon, Rabbit, Tiger	Spring	Wood	East
Snake, Horse, Sheep	Summer	Fire	South
Monkey, Rooster, Dog	Autumn	Metal	West
Ox, Rat, Boar	Winter	Water	North

For greater impact, it is better if they are all using the direction associated with the relevant seasons. This seasonal combination of Spring is East, while the seasonal combination of Summer is South.

The Ox belongs to the seasonal combination of Winter, a combination which strengthens its links with the Rat. Remember that the Rat is both your Secret Friend and your House Soulmate. When an Ox and Rat marry and they have a Boar child, the three of them will form the Trinity of Winter. This means they will not only be inseparable and exceptionally close, but they will also attract the luck of abundance to the family, especially during the winter season!

OX WITH RAT (Excellent)
Rat Benefits from Ox's Steadfastness

The Rat and Ox have a very special relationship being secret friends, soul mates and part of the seasonal trinity that creates the abundance of winter seasons. As such, theirs is always a very auspicious union. It is hard to find another pair of animals with this level of compatibility. In 2010, Rat will be stronger than the Ox but it will be the Ox who brings the bulk of good fortune and luck to this relationship.

Here, the sum of them both is better, luckier and more formidable than they could ever be on their own. Jointly, they create the *House of Creativity and Cleverness* and in 2010, the Ox enjoys the *Star of Big Auspicious* brought by the cosmic energy of the 24 Mountains. So while Rat feels amorous and romantic, Ox directs attention to more mundane matters like making a living! In the Year of the Tiger, it is better if this relationship has the Ox being the breadwinner, irrespective of gender.

Whatever the combination between Rat and Ox, there will always be mutual respect and feelings of fondness and warmth. Even as friends, or as siblings, these two people always support one another. They will be there for each other. Two sisters or two brothers of these animal signs grow up extraordinarily close. The Rat and Ox in their twenties were both born in years when the heavenly stem is Wood and their luck in 2010 complement one another; but it is Ox who will chase after success with greater passion. The Ox is strongly supportive of its Rat partner, but might get impatient with Rat's distractedness.

For the Rat and Ox in their thirties, their 2010 luck is exciting and full of promise. Workwise, the Rat has the Midas touch, enjoying superb wealth enhancement possibilities. The Ox is also enjoying a good ride matching Rat's excellent outlook. Both will experience success and financial advancement in 2010, so as a couple, they are on a roll. However, they should watch their health. Be mindful of becoming too indulgent, such as too many late nights. Excessive partying can take its toll.

The Rat and Ox in their forties do not fair well this year. If married, Rat should depend on Ox's judgement. It is important that Rat does not allow his/her wandering eyes to give in to outside temptation; any unfaithful behaviour is sure to have repercussions, and then things become quite sad indeed. The Ox in this relationship should stay alert to developments in his/her personal life and not get too hung up on business and work.

OX WITH OX *(Workable)*
In 2010, This Stubborn Pair Stays Close

In the Year of the Tiger, Ox people benefit most from their sense of discipline and ability to get down to work. These qualities make them appreciate their own kind, making an Ox pairing with Ox relatively workable. Ox people are very egoistic and they value their own judgment above others. They can also be stubborn, but show their best side when they find themselves under pressure or when they are feeling weak or insecure. This is how they could be feeling this year, and it is these underlying fears that will bring two Ox people together.

Ox people are always closest to their loved ones when faced with challenges and difficulties. Under duress they will surprise even themselves with their own ingenuity. This is when an Ox will find another Ox person vibrant and exciting, so in 2010, with the Tiger bringing quite a fierce year and with conditions being rather challenging, the Ox will find its own sign very attractive indeed. Their time together will be stimulating and filled with animated discussion. There is no time for boredom to set in. The danger here lies in their inherently strong nature. Because they are both strong people, relations can easily become aggravating. The Ox finds being romantic a little tiresome. In a longer term relationship between two

Ox people, love can easily dissipate. The good news is that Ox people do not give up easily especially not on something as serious as a long term relationship, so in terms of staying power, two Ox people stand a good chance of going all the way.

In 2010, the Ox couple can become impatient, intolerant and easily tired out. It is not a very conducive time for them both and the main thing keeping them together is the need to stay united in the face of a challenging year.

The year will thankfully move quite fast for them as the success luck of all Ox born people is good in 2010. This suggests that the year should be filled with more positives than negatives, especially for the 37 year old Water Ox when there is excellent financial luck as well. Should two of them be together, it is likely they will find the year conducive to their relationship. The Ox in their twenties could find themselves quarrelling over money as their financial luck is at an all time low. Worrying about money will be what drives them apart, but the good news is that there is success and health luck to make the year less difficult. On balance, a pair of Ox may be stubborn, but they will stay close and happy in 2010.

OX WITH TIGER (*Indifference*)
No Real Interest from Either Side

There are no special ties between these two signs and in the astrological scheme of things, zodiac relationships need some kind of link for any pairing to really work on a long term basis. These are two signs well known for being strong characters. It is not surprising that they should really not have much interest in one another unless they happen to be brought into each other's orbit by some shared passion, sport or hobby. Even then, any linking up will be quite temporary.

> In 2010, both have their own interests. Ox is particularly listless and not interested. Afflicted by the illness star and feeling the effects of low energy, Ox cannot be bothered to play the sexy siren (in the case of the Lady Ox) or the eager suitor (in the case of guys). They are simply not very interested in romance this year.

In 2010, the Ox is definitely not interested in love, marriage or in the Tiger person! If already hitched to a Tiger, they will tolerate each other, but there is little real interest in each other. This is a couple distracted by other things. Physically, they are not at their best, as both are vulnerable to the illness star. This hits the Ox harder than it does the Tiger. The year does not have anything puling them apart, so these two signs will not see each other as adversaries. There is no special animosity or enmity emanating towards one another, but they are also not "buddies" in that there won't be any easy camaraderie between them.

They have different personalities and their thought processes are dissimilar. Ox people are much better focused than Tiger people. One is a domestic animal, the other a creature of the wild! So these are two people with little in common.

In 2010, the Ox and Tiger in their twenties are surprisingly open to the idea of a relationship between them. Their heavenly stems are also conducive with the Tiger being Fire and the older Ox being Wood, so here the Tiger could find the Ox attractive enough to kindle some interest. Any relationship started may not last, but for as long as it does, they should have a good time!

As for the Ox/Tiger pairing in their thirties, the Water Ox has little time for the Wood Tiger, being too busy pursuing their career or other work-related matters.

OX WITH RABBIT *(Intolerant)*
Intolerance Sets In

The Ox in 2010 has neither interest nor very much time for the Rabbit. Both have their own distractions and there are few opportunities for them to come together. What little they had in common last year has fizzled out, so this is a pair that are unlikely to become an ongoing couple.

> In the Year of the Tiger, the Ox finds the Rabbit's quiet disposition annoying. Impatience sets in between those tied to one another in marriage. Hence where in past years they could have had some kind of relationship together, this year there is zero tolerance; indeed the Ox will find the mere presence of the Rabbit to be a source of annoyance.

These two signs appear irritated by even merely being in the same room. They are not astrological enemies but behave as if they are. Much of it stems from the lack of respect for one another. Of the two, it is Ox who is the more negative. Rabbit is happy to avoid meeting altogether as it instinctively knows there are simply too many areas of potential conflict. So Rabbit will leave first.

Ox can be quite unbending and in 2010, is pulled down by a lack of energy and susceptibility to illness. Its Life Force is weak and its inner chi essence is also low, so a mood of pervasive negativity makes Ox stubborn, easily finding fault with others. The gentler side of Ox is buried deep. In 2010 Rabbit's gentle and soft spoken demeanor will annoy rather than placate Ox, so best if they stay apart.

All of this merely reflects the natural antipathy between these two signs based on zodiac analysis. Differences in their personal life goals, values and aspirations are wide ranging. Rabbit is an indulgent person who enjoys the fine things in life, while Ox is more practical and down to earth, being a no-nonsense type of person. Ox is also a workaholic bent on making a mark on the world. In 2010, this aspect is in evidence and because the year is tough, Ox has a short fuse! Rabbit on the other hand is relaxed, blessed by the celestial star of 6 which brings luck from heaven. There is no room for Ox in Rabbit's world! One can say that Rabbit is moving on and coping with the Tiger Year splendidly. It pursues other interests that take it far away from the world that Ox prefers. Best then for these two signs to go their own separate ways.

OX WITH DRAGON (*Lethargic*)
Just Can't Get Moving

The two powerful signs of Ox and Dragon find it hard to get their act together, not just in love but in other areas as well. Something seems to be holding them back and there is a certain lethargy that hangs heavy on them. This affects their attitudes towards each other, and also the way they respond to others. The year is quite good for Ox, but less kind to the Dragon, and this could be a problem. Dragon does not appreciate appearing less successful. More to the point, both have very negative readings in their horoscope element charts. Ox and Dragon both register strong negatives in the category of Life Force and inner chi essence. These have a significant impact on their attitudes and behaviour in general.

Ox normally finds Dragon dynamic and exciting, and horoscope indications suggest that these two can inspire each other to great heights when the energy of the year is right, but this does not seem to be happening in 2010. The Tiger Year is casting gloom on their relationship.

Should you be a couple already married, you must not take anything said between you to heart. Better not to respond to negative remarks as these will just be carelessly thrown out statements that are not meant to hurt. Response of any kind will only lead to a turning away and will not improve matters. Unlike last year when everything was a lot brighter, this year, things are simply not the same.

In 2010, the exhilarating feeling that comes with having soaring ambitions is sorely missing. There is a sad lack of energy and unless you both pull up your socks, there is danger you will simply allow the year to pass without you getting anywhere either as a couple or singly. Those in a partnership together must try hard to motivate themselves. Ox has always been very good at doing this. And because there is an underlying sense of respect for each other, Ox can pull Dragon up as well, so if it is worth it to do so, you should make an effort.

In 2010, Ox can make big strides in work and career. Dragon encounters too many disappointments. Only the 34 year old Fire Dragon experiences good financial luck; others are less lucky. So Ox will set the tone for this relationship. But it is Dragon who provides the vision, creativity and courage. If they can pull themselves together, they can work well as a team. Their skills are complementary and it benefits them to strengthen their resolve in the Year of the Tiger.

OX WITH SNAKE *(High Energy)*
Ox Has Hard Time Keeping Up

These two signs are incredibly compatible. You are comfortable and relaxed with each other and are so in sync you can almost read each other's minds. You love the same things, admire the same people and are inspired by similar ambitions. There is excellent communication and rapport between you.

This is not surprising because the Ox is an ally of the Snake, and the two of you form a powerful Alliance of Allies with the Rooster. These three signs pride themselves on being sharp, quick witted and intellectually inclined. They do not suffer fools gladly and have a rather high opinion of themselves. So Ox has quite a lot in common with Snake this way.

The only problem is that Snake has very high energy in 2010 and Ox finds it can barely keep up. In terms of everything, Snake outshines Ox, but most importantly, Snake's Life Force is simply too strong for Ox to measure up. Physically and mentally, Snake will tend to be sharper, quicker and even more popular. Oh dear!

Snake's inner confidence is also excellent and Ox might wilt in the glare of Snake's mesmerizing personality. Others are drawn to the Snake, who will hold court this year with style and verve. Ox will feel inferior and be hit by pangs of inadequacy and this is sure to affect their relationship.

If they are married, jealousy could create strains for them. Should they be partners in business, or colleagues at work, their team work could suffer.

This is a year when Ox needs to sit back and let Snake shine. When your partner is on a roll, rejoice and be happy. This will take much of the tension out of your relationship. It is more Snake's year than yours, so try to be magnanimous.

Let your mutual respect help you through the year. Also have faith in Snake's sense of loyalty and kindness. As the one with less energy, you the Ox should allow Snake to take the lead and call the shots. Do not belittle Snake's achievements in any way or throw out caustic remarks, as this is the surest way of making Snake turn away. Instead, rejoice in Snake's good fortune and be there if needed. This is a year when both of you have your share of setbacks, but there are real benefits for you to stay close, so make the effort to do so.

OX WITH HORSE *(Exciting)*
Riding High with Horse

This represents the attraction of opposites, the free-spirited Horse with the practical, disciplined Ox. There are obvious differences between this pair and few similarities. This year, Ox continues to be strongly attracted to the charming, charismatic Horse. Ox becomes engagingly smitten and will behave quite out of character, like a love starved teenager. In this relationship, Horse dominates. This is because Horse has tough attributes and exhibits strong characteristics in 2010, exuding self confidence and vitality, spurred on by a year that is both auspicious and friendly. It seems its ally the Tiger brings goodies to the Horse, transforming it into an exciting individual indeed.

Whether or not anything started with Horse can last depends on many factors, not least Ox's capacity to endure a relationship where the partner has so little staying power. They rarely fail to achieve what they set out to do and definitely have more wins than losses in the love department. Horse personifies nobility, class and chic, attributes Ox finds irresistible. So yes, a friendship can definitely develop into something deeper and even survive the test of time. Horse is at its best in 2010, and Ox will have a fair bit of competition. You will need to keep jealous urges under control.

Ox is generally solid, down-to-earth and pragmatic, on the surface appearing to lack the spirit of adventure that characterizes the Horse. But first impressions can sometimes be deceptive. Under the right conditions, and inspired by the right person, Ox can be as brave as any cowboy! Give the Ox a reason to be adventurous and watch it surprise you by climbing the Himalayas or swimming the deepest oceans. But not this year! In 2010 alas, Ox is lacking in the energy stakes. It will be a case of the spirit being willing but the body being insufficiently strong.

The main thing for the Ox to know is that underlying all that bravado, Horse has an insecure streak, needing a great deal of reassurance.

Ox could discover that Horse can be fickle, refusing to be bound by conventions, chaffing at the bit and capable of just taking off without warning. In the long run, Ox cannot find stable happiness with Horse. But in 2010, Ox is in no position to stop any relationship with Horse being nicely hooked! The attraction is just too strong and Horse's vitality is irresistible. Ox does not have the strength to walk away. Perhaps it is better to stick around and enjoy – after all, who said relationships have to be long term? Better to take things one day at a time and go with the flow.

OX WITH SHEEP *(Insensitive)*
In 2010, Double Negatives Repel

The Ox and Sheep have no attraction for each other, let alone love or have thoughts of a serious commitment. In Chinese astrology, these two are natural adversaries who have little time or sympathy for one another. In 2010, they are equally balanced in terms of what the year has in store for them. They are both Earth people, so there is a down-to-earth aspect to their personalities, but because they are both Yin Earth, the tendency is for them to be constantly negative. And being both negative there is no attraction, and instead they just naturally repel each other. They have few nice things to say about each other should they be in a relationship. It is all very adversarial.

> In 2010, these two signs have to endure some tough afflictions. The Sheep is afflicted by the *wu wang* which brings misfortune luck, while the Ox is plagued by the illness star. These afflictions do nothing to soften them up for one another so 2010 does not look good for this pair at all.

Instead of helping one another, they will be aggravating and annoying, adding salt to injury. In fact, this can be the year they split, as any differences between them simply do not go away and will just linger on. Any misunderstanding between Ox and Sheep will get magnified quite easily.

In 2010, Ox gets impatient with Sheep's troubles. Being hit by the *wu wang* is not easy, and since this is a major affliction, Sheep does not take kindly to Ox's lack of sympathy. So while Ox is busy changing the world with its grand plans, Sheep prefers to continue its resting mode of last year. Sheep stays quiet and low key and will walk away from Ox if they are in a relationship. This is probably a good thing as the longer term outlook does not look promising to either.

If you are in an Ox/Sheep pairing, you may have endured a difficult time with each other. Living with, or being married to your Zodiac enemy is definitely no fun, and may even hurt you. There is an underlying insensitivity between these two for which there is no real cure. It is better to get out of the relationship if it is causing you pain and suffering.

If you have tolerated each other for many years, there could be aspects of your paht chee charts that make you compatible and if so, let things be. Nevertheless it is always a good idea to wear some kind of **mantra protection** if you are married to your astrological enemy. And place a large **twirling crystal ball** on your coffee table to enhance of good harmony vibes.

OX WITH MONKEY *(Awesome)*
Mutual Admiration Fuels This Pair

These two remarkable characters continue to find one another attractive in 2010, so if you are dating a Monkey, by all means go for it!

There is something quite splendid about the way Ox reacts to Monkey, because despite them being very different, they are attracted to each other. They differ in the way they think, and the way they arrive at conclusions, but these are two people who will find time for each other. There is respect and a feeling of simpatico between them and any chi vibrations generated are positive.

Ox and Monkey will create a mutual admiration society in 2010, although this is a year that favors Monkey a great deal more than Ox. Just remember that their admiration for one another is based on totally different bases. The end result is the same, but how they get there mentally is what is different.

In their world, there is always room for contrary opinions. Their world views are not the same, Ox being a lot more straightforward and less crafty than the Monkey. But both are visionaries capable of lifting themselves into space and looking down at the world below them from the same perspective yet seeing different things.

The Monkey is saddled with the *wu wang* affliction this year and it also has the unpredictable *Sui Po Star*, but its horoscope is strong and full of inner vitality, so in 2010, it forges ahead with little hesitation. This is an animal sign that is not afraid of the Tiger, and of course, its energy levels support this bravado approach. Ox will be a great deal more circumspect as this is a person who moves warily as a matter of habit.

Ox is drawn to Monkey's energy and will view some of the decisions taken by Monkey to be nothing short of awe inspiring. From the third quarter onwards, starting in August, Monkey will make one swinging decision after another, leaving Ox breathless and panting to keep up!

Against this scenario arises a grand attraction. Love is in the air for this couple. The Tiger Year is as powerful for the Monkey as it was last year. For Ox, the year is a little lacking in terms of support energy, so will need to depend on Monkey. Right into January 2011, this pair will be on a roller coaster high despite their afflictions; more so if they are properly protected with the right kind of remedies. This couple should be able to find happiness with one another.

OX WITH ROOSTER *(Supportive)*
Rooster Gives Ox A Boost

The Ox likes anyone born in the Rooster year, and
the feeling is splendidly mutual. Not only are they
members of the same Alliance of Allies (with the
Snake) but they also think alike, being mentally in
sync most of the way. They have similar aspirations
when it comes to making their way in the world.
These are two signs that are no nonsense types. They
see this in each other the moment they meet, so they
easily forge a powerful connection. The compatibility
between them is obvious instantly as they naturally
gravitate to one another. There is no need even for
anyone to introduce them.

> They work well in the same team, so career-wise
> they each benefit directly from the other, and also
> from their positive "can-do" approach to the world.
> The Ox and Rooster together are fearless and will
> tell a great cock and bull story anytime if it will get
> them ahead of the competition.

They are folks that see humour in situations that
others miss. They do not take themselves too seriously.
But theirs is a high humor! This is the underlying
basis of their strong friendship. Between them is a
bond that is hard to break. So Ox, if you are eyeing
a Rooster as a potential mate, by all means go for it.

Whatever your intentions, the response is certain to be positive.

As business partners they are also successful. In 2010, Ox is handicapped by its low energy levels and also the occasional crisis of confidence. Physically also, Ox is being afflicted by the illness star. Rooster on the other hand is riding high this year with strong vitality levels and also blessed by the triumphant winning star. Ox should influence the Rooster and tell it to slow down.

The Tiger Year will challenge their resources and staying power but as a team they can ride through with no problem. They do not give up easily and are ruled more by their heads than by their hearts, so logic and good rationale will influence their actions. Ox and Rooster are very practical people who are not easy to fool, and since they do not get carried away or give in to impulsive decision making, they should do OK.

Their approach to life is purposeful and confident and they can face whatever the year brings with no problem at all. In 2010, the Rooster is on a high. Luck is at its maximum level so Ox can hitch a ride on the Rooster bandwagon. There is both success and money in the charts, so this pair will find that 2010 works out well for them as a couple. As long as Ox gives way to Rooster this year, all should go well.

OX WITH DOG *(Successful)*
Low Energy But Oh So Auspicious

The Ox and Dog is a pairing that holds out the promise of success, especially in 2010 when both enjoy auspicious luck. In terms of being able to get along, they are not unsuited to each other, although they also do not get along like a house on fire. Theirs is a restrained relationship although there is a comfort level that they find with one another. They have a friendship between them, and easy banter and communication flow freely.

> The Ox finds Dog very accommodating and easy to live with. It will never be a strenuous relationship between this pair and of course, the Dog is also a very amiable person not given to strong opinions. In the Year of the Tiger, these are qualities that make Dog a very lovable person.

For the couple to go deeper into a serious relationship, much depends on their lifestyle and on the values they grew up with. There is good potential for them to be close if they come from similar backgrounds and if their folks mix in the same social circles. Educational background also contributes to their relationship.

In 2010, Ox and Dog have equally low, in fact negative, energy levels. Their Life Force and inner chi essence make them light eared to outside influence, especially the tough Ox who is not so tough this year, being vulnerable to the illness star. The Dog on the other hand enjoys good fortune despite its low vitality. Its home location is visited by the 9 star which magnifies all good luck coming its way. But whether Dog can or will help Ox is another matter.

Ox can put Dog off by being too correct and too rigid. In 2010, Dog will want solace and comfort; many things can go wrong not least of which is the Dog's need for a shoulder occasionally. This is because both its life force and inner essence are low.

The problem is that Ox is in the same boat, so both sides must understand the need for sensitivity to each other's troubles. Here, living in a state of mindfulness is vital to their staying together. It is the natural warm responses that will bring them closer. Lukewarm words of support are not good enough for either. They need to go deeper in their relationship if it is to get anywhere this year.

Those already married are advised to be perceptive of each other's hidden problems this year. The best month for Ox will be January 2011 and for Dog, good fortune begins in October.

OX WITH BOAR *(Nonchalant)*
Cannot Find Common Ground

This pair has little in common and should they meet and come together, they find it hard to establish a comfortable feeling with each other. They cannot find the rhythm as there seems to be very little by way of shared passions or hobbies. So they tend to leave each other quite cold.

When they meet, they are laid back, with both likely adopting an air of indifference. They are not putting on an act. This is a reflection of the lack of excitement between an Ox and a Boar. It is possible for them to be friends, but rarely will a love relationship bring out any excitement. They cannot generate much passion for one another. Any relationship they have is best characterized as a terrible indifference that makes this a boring relationship.

In 2010, Boar appears to have a better year than Ox, with life force and inner chi energy at average levels when compared to the negative readings for Ox. As a result, they are unable to be in sync with each other. Ox will focus on work and end up ignoring Boar most of the time. So beyond the first five minutes, these two people will have precious little to chat about.

Another problem is that they are not very interested in each other's opinions. Here it is not just about being good or bad for each other; there is just no spark ignited between them. Nothing that one does will stimulate the other, so they find each other rather dull. Those who just met will probably split after a couple of outings.

Humor is also missing, so a challenging Tiger Year is sure to be tough for this couple. They are too serious, unable to use laughter to get them through the year. Both of you deserve better than to be stuck with someone so unsuitable for you! The advice is to focus on how to make the most of the year on your own. It should not be necessary to depend on a partner, and in any case, this is a year when both the Boar and Ox work better as loners.

Setting time aside for contemplation and serious strategic thinking is more worthwhile. For those already married to each other, try to find a comfort zone and then get on with your life.

2010 is not a great year for Boar as energy levels are negative. The Boar is lethargic about many relationships and will need something special to galvanize him. It is unlikely that the year will oblige.

Part 3
Monthly Outlook

The Ox person is inconvenienced by the *Side Tai Sui* this year thus you will need a **pair of Pi Yao**. The Ox is also vulnerable to illness, so pay more attention to your health. If something does not feel right, get it checked out. There are some good indications with the *Star of Big Auspicious* bringing some excellent luck but you will need to stay strong in order to enjoy this luck.

Display **Acala's Ball and Disc** in the NE to boost personal strength and resilience. The year does not start out great, so it is better to stay low key in the first half of the year. Things improve by midyear and August brings some bonanza luck. October helps those of you in positions of authority and power. New romances blossom in March and December.

1ST MONTH
February 4th - March 5th 2010

POSTPONE MAKING BIG DECISIONS

The year does not start off so good so it is best to be careful. Play it safe and avoid taking risks. Misfortunes could cause accidents and possible loss. Carry or wear a **wu lou amulet** to stave off illness. Postpone making big decisions, especially when there is much at stake. Hard work is the only way to make money this month; avoid taking any gambles and watch who you fraternize with. Mixing with the wrong crowd could cause you to lose more than you bargained for. Business could suffer loss, so put safeguards in place. This is also not a good month to travel, so avoid doing so if you can.

WORK & CAREER – *Stay Alert*

You're in a vulnerable position and good luck can reverse itself very quickly. Unexpected hiccups interrupt your usually calm demeanor. This is a time when you cannot afford to make mistakes, but allowing stress to overcome you will only make things worse. Be more meticulous with your work because anything sub-standard will be found out and pointed out quickly. Someone you have angered in the past could plot their petty revenge, so it is wise to watch your back. Make sure you have all your protective enhancers in place. Keep a **Rooster** figurine on your desk to counter office politics; the Rooster is also your horoscope ally, so tapping on its energy will also strengthen much needed friendship luck. If you are in a managerial position, you should also have a **Ru Yi** enhancer to ensure you have the support of those who work under you.

BUSINESS – *Watch Your Wallet*

It is easy to lose money in a month when your luck is under par. Be more careful with spending and do not think of investing at a time like this. Avoid entering into new joint ventures or other alliances, especially if it involves money. Even long-time friends and steadfast business acquaintances could fall out with you at a time like this.

If you need to enter into any new contracts or agreements, try to anticipate all eventualities. It is better not to sign anything this month. Hold off till next month when your luck improves. When it comes to financial matters, things may not be as straightforward as they seem. Steer clear of any temptation to fiddle with numbers in an attempt to improve your tax situation. You could be doing something illegal without knowing, subjecting you to problems and headaches later on.

LOVE & RELATIONSHIPS – *Curb Your Ego*

Don't let envy or jealousy get the better of you. You may find yourself in a competitive situation with your spouse or partner, but working together and nurturing a positive relationship is more important than coming out on top. Personal pride could be your undoing, so learn to have more humility. There is plenty of good that can come out of this month as long as you don't let your own self-importance get in the way. For Ox persons who are single, this is not the best time to pursue romantic conquests. You may find yourself overly emotional and scare potential partners away!

PERSONAL HEALTH – *Rest Up*

Falling sick could become a real inconvenience. Keep yourself healthy by avoiding overwork. Maintain a sensible diet. If you feel you are coming down with something, give yourself time to recuperate. Trying to "push through" an illness will only make things worse.

EDUCATION – *Shrug Off Criticisms*

You may be in for some criticism from a teacher this month. Don't take things personally or let it affect your psyche. Develop some strength of character and don't let your own self worth be determined by other people's opinion of you. Things will improve by leaps and bounds next month.

2ND MONTH
March 6th - April 4th 2010

CREATIVITY LEVELS ARE HIGH

Your luck improves from last month and you find your creativity levels at a high. Those in fields of work or study requiring original thought will find it easy to think up brilliant new ideas. This is also a particularly good month for young Ox persons in school. Romance is in the air for young couples in love. The downside to an otherwise happy month could come in the form of mother-in-law trouble in the home. If you live with extended family in the house, there could be disharmony in the home. To counter this, display **six round crystal balls** in the living or family room. This will ensure peace in the home. For Ox in business, this is a promising month.

WORK & CAREER – *Creating Consensus*

Relationships go well this month, so put more effort into cultivating a good rapport with your boss and those you work with. Use this time to make friends and build your network. You are adept at sorting out problems and could find others using you as a sounding board. Brainstorming goes well and you make a valuable member on any team. If you have good ideas, share them! Others take you seriously and genuinely welcome your suggestions. You are also in the fortunate position of not appearing a threat to your co-workers. The competitive aspect of your worklife is subdued, making things much more pleasant at the office. Use this time to further yourself. There are also good prospects for promotion.

BUSINESS – *Good for Sales*

You have a natural affinity with others this month, so make it a point to focus on areas which involve dealing with other people. Winning over new clients will prove easier than usual and you begin to really enjoy your work. You could find a new calling this month. Go with your heart. If you are enjoying what you are doing, chances are you will do an even better job of it. You have real flair for pitching your ideas to others and getting them just as excited as you are. Your mind is also sharper than usual, which adds to your ability to stay focused to see things through to successful completion. Make the most of this month; you can get a lot of good work done.

LOVE & RELATIONSHIPS – *Get Hitched*

This is an especially good month for marriages and proposals. Nuptials held this month bode well for the future, so if you are looking for a good time to tie the knot this year, consider holding your wedding this month. For Ox already married, put more focus on spending quality time with your other half. You could discover new things to share that draw you even closer to one another. For the single Ox, there are plenty of opportunities for love and romance. Enjoy them!

FAMILY & FRIEND – *Staying in Touch*

This is a good time to look up distant cousins and other relatives. Touch base with them while you're feeling sociable. Apart from good company, building up your support team will be important for you this year. You may receive a call from an old friend this month. Make an effort to keep in touch. Someone you thought you'd left behind long ago will resurface in your life and may well become an important factor in your world soon.

EDUCATION – *Prolific Month*

Academic study and knowledge accumulation is prolific; there is a lot you can learn if you set your mind to it. You benefit from clarity of thought and find it easy to grasp new concepts. New ideas come easily. Learn to share them and use them to get ahead in the classroom. Keep yourself on top of things by starting your assignments as soon as they are set, instead of just before the deadline. This way the topic at hand will still be fresh in your mind. If you make this a habit, you'll find you always have plenty of time left to fit in other activities which interest you.

3RD MONTH
April 5th - May 5th 2010

MISUNDERSTANDING BETWEEN FRIENDS

This month the Ox person faces risk of severe arguments and misunderstandings which could result in bad consequences. There is disharmony among friends and acquaintances. Quarrels may surface at work or in personal friendships. Court cases and litigation is possible. There is also risk of backstabbing by people whom you trust. Don't rely on others this month. It is better to take charge of your own life, so if anything goes wrong, there is less chance of dispute over whose fault it is. Avoid confrontation, and try to lie low. When you feel your temper starting to simmer, try to take your mind off things by engaging in a relaxing activity or sport.

WORK & CAREER – *Short Fuse*

Avoid losing your cool at the workplace. If you let anger get the better of you, you will end up the loser. Nobody appreciates an explosive personality, and although you may use it as a tactic to get things done, this month you could push it a bit too far. Control your temper. Avoid landing yourself in sticky situations where you raise the probability of a dispute.

It may be better for you to go on holiday this month, and take a break to relax and unwind. Avoid lengthy discussion-type meetings; if you have no choice, limit your contribution and learn to recognize when you've said too much.

BUSINESS — *Disharmony Causes Problems*

Don't be surprised if the office is in turmoil this month. You will need to draw on the best of your people skills to keep everyone motivated. Misunderstandings between co-workers are likely, and as a boss you might well find yourself caught up in between. Put more effort into calming nerves and smoothing out inter-office relationships. Tension of this kind could set back productivity significantly. For greater harmony in the office, display **six large smooth crystal balls** in the NE sector of the office.

LOVE & RELATIONSHIPS — *Count to Ten*

Not a great month for love. You tend to be more bad tempered than usual, and your arrogance could put people off. Learn some humility and you will be much better liked. For the Ox at the dating stage of their relationships, be careful not to scare your potential partner away with your egoistic tendencies. Make it a habit to think of your partner first. This will help you in your pursuit of love, but this is not the best of months to formalize anything. Keep things casual and leave the big moves for later when your luck improves.

FAMILY – *Take Deep Breaths*

There is antagonistic energy in the home between yourself and other family members. This is not the best of times to discuss serious issues; you are likely to disagree, leading to tempers flaring. Make an extra effort to be understanding. The more considerate you are to others, the easier you will find this month. Arguments with family members threaten to cloud your mind in other areas of your life, because the people with the power to upset you most are those closest to you. Place an **urn of still water** in the NE sector.

SCHOOL & EDUCATION – *Motivation the Key*

Ox in school benefit from the guidance and close supervision of a responsible adult or mentor figure. As long as you can keep motivated, you can make this month a productive one. Don't hold grudges against friends you feel have betrayed you or let you down; you may not have the whole story and may be wrongly judging somebody. It is better to give them the benefit of the doubt.

4TH MONTH
May 6th - June 5th 2010

ILLNESS CAUSES WORRIES

Illness vibes bring danger to the Ox person this month. The negative energies of the year are magnified with a matching illness star flying into the sector of the Ox, bringing the strong possibility of minor ailments becoming more serious. Take your health seriously this month. If there is something not quite right, check it out. But avoid hospitals if possible, as over exposure to locations of yin energy could exacerbate the unlucky effects of your chart stars this month. Try not to sleep in the NE sector. If you bedroom is located here, move out of that room for the month.

WORK & CAREER – *Staying Low Key*

Cut yourself some slack at work this month. Allow yourself an easy day if you're feeling under the weather. Don't schedule anything too important for this month. Your luck is down and you don't want to let the rest of your team down. If you work in a very structured environment, it is best to stick to the rules. Striving for change or being in any way rebellious threatens to backfire. Keep a low profile and focus on your core activities and doing them well. Appearing overly ambitious right now could be more harmful than helpful. Beware jealous colleagues and office politics. Invest in a **Rooster** figurine for your desk if you don't already have one. This will stem office intrigues targeted at you.

BUSINESS – *Watch Your Cash Flow*

Stress may get to you this month, especially if you are trying to take on too much. Learn to recognize when you are getting mentally exhausted and take a break! Refresh your mind by ensuring you have a life outside of the office. This is an unlucky period to invest. Better to conserve your cash and protect your cash flow. Unexpected expenses may crop up, so be prepared for it. If the need arises, be prepared to cut your losses rather than hold out and end up losing more. Think big rather than small, and stay brave and optimistic through tough times. Things improve next month.

LOVE & RELATIONSHIPS – *Getting Cosy*

Luck in love looks brighter this month. If you're in a relationship, you will see yourself growing noticeably closer to your partner. Thinking along the same wavelength comes easily, and unlike with last month's quarrelsome tendencies, difficult issues are absent from your relationship this month.

Enjoy this peaceful time by making more time to spend with each other. The more you engage yourselves in meaningful conversation, the better your relationship will get and the stronger the bond between you will grow.

HEALTH & WELLNESS – *Get a Wu Lou*

This month it is extremely important to look after your health. The illness star in your chart gets magnified, bringing risk of serious illness and infection. If you are at all worried, get yourself checked out. And if you are not confident with one doctor, get a second opinion. Display a **brass wu lou** by your bedside to drive away the illness vibes, and wear one as a pendant or carry as a charm for added protection. Wearing **gold jewellery** and whites and metallic colours will also help you healthwise this month.

Wearing the longevity symbol in gold is excellent for the Ox person this month, when the illness star gets strengthened by the month's influences.

EDUCATION – *A Level Time*

Don't take on too much this month as you suffer from a general lack of energy. It is better to do a few things well than many things with mediocrity.

5TH MONTH
June 6th - July 6th 2010

BUSINESS & WORK LUCK IS GOOD

Things improve significantly this month. There are plenty of opportunities to sink your teeth into and you see obstacles in your life lifted as if by magic. Things move along smoothly in all areas of your life and you find simple solutions to problems that have been festering. Be deliberate with your choices this month. Once you have decided on something, stick with it. Trust your instincts. Business and work luck in particular is good, so this is a time when you can expect to make good headway in your professional life.

WORK & CAREER — *Upward Mobility*

You can expect a few changes at work this month. You may be promoted or transferred to another department, your job scope and nature of your responsibilities may change, but it will be for the better. Even if a promotion does not come with an immediate raise in salary, you can expect to enjoy the monetary fruits of your accomplishments in the near future.

A new colleague that joins the team may change the dynamics at the workplace, but try and be warm and

welcoming. He or she may make a useful ally later on.
Income luck is promising. Boost career luck with a
Monkey on an Elephant in the North sector.

BUSINESS – *Seeing the Big Picture*

As business luck is good, this is a promising time to be
daring with new ideas. Go with ideas that tickle you.
If something can capture your imagination, you will
be able to make it work to capture the imagination
of others as well. Be hands on with your business
operations this month. Don't be too picky over the tiny
details. Focus on broad strategy rather than the nitty
gritty. Operational issues will sort themselves out once
you work out a comprehensive overall strategy. For Ox
people thinking of venturing out on their own to set
up a business, this could be a good time to do it. Tap
on alliances made in the past. If you look, there will be
people willing and able to help you.

LOVE & RELATIONSHIPS – *Change of Heart*

Expect a dramatic month when it comes to matters
of the heart. There is potential for both major highs
and lows. You could fall deeper in love with someone
special, or out of love completely. If it is the latter, do
not despair because things will improve before you
know it. A brief spell of pain could open the door to a
lot of happiness in the not too distant future. For the
married Ox, don't assume your spouse understands you

and knows what you want. This is a time to be more verbal with your needs if you want the satisfaction you feel you deserve from your relationship. While you may want to satisfy your own desires, don't forget those of your partners. It will feel so much better if you are both mutually satisfied.

FAMILY & HOME LIFE — *Staying Connected*

This is a good time to give your home a makeover. Clean the house of clutter. All things that are no longer needed should be thrown out or given away to people who need them. You need to regularly move the Chi in your living space to create good energies around you. Throwing out old and unwanted items will make way for new things to come into your life. This is also a good time to repaint and redecorate. Buy a new piece of furniture and remove an old piece. Try some with auspicious carvings on them to bring lucky Chi into the home.

A Monkey on an Elephant in the North will bring excellent career luck.

6TH MONTH
July 7th - Aug 7th 2010

COULD SUFFER FROM CARELESSNESS

This month is characterized by a lack of energy. The illness star 2 is magnified by the number 9 multiplying star, bringing an all around weakness of chi energy. Illness shows no signs of easing. Business suffers from carelessness. Lethargy may send you into an unproductive inertia. Kick start your luck by combating low energy levels with exercise and a healthy diet. Take your health and wellness seriously. Get enough sleep but don't overdo the sleep. Too much can become as bad as too little. If you lack enthusiasm in life, this may be a good time to try a new hobby or activity. Injecting some newfound excitement into your daily routine could make a huge difference.

WORK & CAREER – *Eye on Strategy*

If you're in a competitive work environment, you may have to be a little cunning to get ahead this month. Stay on the ball at work because careless mistakes will be picked up quickly. There is no qualms when it comes to placing the blame, and if you don't defend yourself, you could well find yourself being made the scapegoat. The strong-willed among you will be the ones who do well this month. No need to be too humble or nice. This month a little bit of grit and determination is what you need. But don't be impulsive with your actions. Think before you act to make sure any move you make is a carefully calculated one. As Ox people are great strategists, this should not be a problem for you as long as you keep it in mind.

BUSINESS – *Be Meticulous*

Business luck is poor, but negative outcomes usually result from carelessness rather than market conditions. While market demand could be weak, it will not be the main factor deciding how well you do. Pay attention to details. Boost productivity by making sure everyone is pulling their weight. This could be a time when you need to up your motivation pep talks with the staff. Teamwork is important, and a well coordinated team effort is the best chance of fending off the negative chi that threatens the Ox person this month. If you are in a partnership, it may be best to leave the running of day-to-day matters to a non-Ox partner.

LOVE & RELATIONSHIPS – *Staying Cool*

Luck in love is better than luck elsewhere, so make this aspect of your life count. Things happen quickly on the romance front. However, you don't react well to pressure and if someone wants to take things too fast, you may start to back off. Gently let them know if you're uncomfortable with anything. If they are the right person for you, they will understand. It would help if you're a little less defensive. Open up your heart to love and there could be something really special awaiting you this month.

HEALTH – *Watch that Bug!*

You're more susceptible to catching viruses and falling ill this month. Avoid exposing yourself to infectious diseases and overly crowded places this month. This is also not a great month for travel or pursuit of dangerous sports or activities. Avoid the NE sector; if your bedroom is located here, try to move to another room for the month and arm yourself with a Wu Lou amulet. Elderly Ox people especially should be more careful.

FAMILY – *Walking Time*

This is a good time to spend with family members. There may be important family issues to resolve. If there are pressing matters you have been putting off, this is a good time to deal with them. Make time for those closest to you even if work is demanding a lot of your time. If you manage your life in an organized manner, there is a lot that can be accomplished. This is a fertile time to rekindle weakening ties with certain members of your family.

7TH MONTH
Aug 8th - Sept 7th 2010

SUM-OF-TEN BRINGS GOOD FORTUNE

This is an excellent recovery month. Sickness shows signs of improving. Wealth luck benefits those in business. There is workplace harmony and new friendships thrive. The sum-of-ten in your chart brings tremendous good fortune, so if there are any important occasions you are planning this year, this is a good month to pick. Excellent for weddings, product launches, signing of agreements and moving in to a new home. The monthly star combines with the annual star to form an incredible combination bringing completeness into your life. You can thus afford to be bolder and take more risks knowing that Lady Luck is on your side. This is also a good month for charitable pursuits, as the more you give, the more you get back in return.

WORK & CAREER – *Excellent Time*

At work you are given the chance to work on things you are really good at, thus giving you a good chance to shine. Your talent, hard work and efforts will be recognized and rewarded. For some, a promotion or income increase come their way; for others the improvement may be more subtle but will be there nevertheless. Good things come to those who wait, so don't become impatient as you progress up the career ladder. Ox people make natural leaders, and this month you may just get that chance to display your leadership potential. Seize any opportunity that comes your way and put all your effort into making it count. Playing your cards right now could get you far for the future.

BUSINESS – *Boomtime*

There is significant wealth luck in your chart this month. Ox at the helm of their own businesses will see better sales and profits without having to increase effort or outlay all that much. Actively look for new ways to augment your wealth. There could be a prolific opportunity to diversify. If something feels right to you, do it. This is a month when taking risks bring benefits. Don't be afraid of a gamble as the outcome is likely to be in your favor. However, having said that, don't be overly foolhardy either. There is a fine balance which you will find if you look.

LOVE & RELATIONSHIPS – *Harmonious*

If you make it a point to dominate the relationship this month, you will see your companion falling in with your plans readily and happily. Things you are unhappy about in your relationship should be talked about. If you don't initiate change, nothing will change. And you will be stuck with what you're not happy with. How badly can your partner take it? They may be feeling exactly the same way as you, but like you, hesitant to say anything for fear of rocking the boat. For those who are ready for a commitment, let your partner know. Use your lucky stars to secure that commitment you've been waiting for. If your partner resists, it may just be time to move on to greener pastures.

HOME & FAMILY – *Staying Close*
Family life is hugely fulfilling this month. You feel a deep sense of love for the people closest to you. This is a good month for developing relationships and repairing damaged ones. This is also a good time for improving the home. The best times to undertake redecoration and renovation are during months in which your luck is up. This way, the energy that goes into the remodeling of the house will be extremely positive.

EDUCATION – *An OK Month*
Make the most of your studies this month. You will do well. But don't neglect exercise and other extra curricular activities. The more well rounded you are, the better you will do.

8TH MONTH
Sept 8th - Oct 7th 2010

SOME JEALOUSY FROM OTHERS

Be watchful of the people around you. There is risk of betrayal and money loss. Even the closest of friends could let you down in a month when your luck veers off track this way. If you feel let down by a friend, be big-hearted and learn to let go. But even better is to prevent anything untoward from happening in the first place.

This month, avoid borrowing or lending money, especially from friends. Expect favors granted to you to come with strings attached. There are many obstacles that form to block your success, but these obstacles can be overcome, as long as you remain mentally strong.

WORK & CAREER – *Green Eyed Monster*

Career luck gets hit by jealous moves by colleagues. Don't make anyone from work your bosom pal. Even if you are close to your co-workers, be a bit guarded when sharing personal secrets. Things you say in jest could be taken out of context at the workplace. Office politics could prove depressing and draining, so ensure you have the **Eight Legged Lion** on your table. This will promote harmony at the workplace and spare you from feeling the full brunt of someone's resentment. You can also display your horoscope allies and secret friend – the Rooster, Snake and Rat – in your office, or wear them on a charm bracelet or as jewelry.

BUSINESS – *Arrows & Envy*

Lay low if you are in business. This is a month where the less done the better. There is no need to change the status quo if business is doing well. Keep a low profile so you do not evoke jealousy from competitors. Do not overspend on marketing, as your efforts may not harvest the returns you expect. When dealing with business associates, watch the monetary side carefully. Although there may be no dishonesty intended, there could be mistakes, which result in misunderstandings. It is better to be transparent and open if you want your relationship to stay smooth and problem-free. This is not a good month for important meetings or discussions as you run the risk of saying the wrong things or revealing too much. Let others do the talking. You will gain far more this way.

LOVE & RELATIONSHIPS – *Annoying Each Other*

Do not expect too much out of your relationships this month. There are other things on your mind and you are unlikely to be able to commit yourself fully to a relationship. This may grate on the nerves of your partner, and if he or she is not understanding enough, it could cause some serious rifts between the two of you. Just as you expect your partner to be considerate to your situation, you should do the same. Because things may be stickier than usual, you may have to compromise with each other. Expecting too much from any relationship will only cause you to be disappointed.

PERSONAL SAFETY – *Watch Your Back*

Watch out for the robbery star that plagues your chart this month. Take more precaution when it comes to safety. Carry a **blue rhinoceros and elephant amulet** to ward off risk of robbery and snatch thieves. Avoid operating heavy machinery and do not renovate this month. It is also prudent to be more careful when it comes to home safety. Remember to lock up at night, and don't take any chances when it comes to security issues. Female Ox should avoid venturing out too late at night. and should carry the **Night Spot Protection Amulet** if they have to stay out late.

Eight Legged Lion - a great symbol for creating harmony in your relationships.

9TH MONTH
Oct 8th - Nov 6th 2010

GAIN NEW RESPECT FROM PEERS

This is a month when authority luck returns to you. You gain respect from your peers and see your influence in general increase. This is the same whether in working life or amongst your personal friends. Although you are riding high this month, you can achieve a lot more with the help of others than on your own. Enhance the luck of allies with a figurine of the Four Friends. This will manifest people in your life who are in a position to help you, whether through their skills, wisdom or position. Accept help humbly and graciously. You may have to call on a few favors to get certain things done this month; if you do, go ahead and pick up the phone. If you ask, they are likely to say yes.

WORK & CAREER – *Not Taking Sides*

Your natural leadership skills are quite obvious to those watching and you may be given an opportunity to lead a team this month. A promotion is on the cards, but don't let yourself get impatient. Instead, concentrate on producing work that cannot be faulted. You may get in the middle of a crossfire where someone wants to promote you while someone else does not. Be careful when dealing with your superiors that you do not obviously take sides. You may be more loyal to some people than others, but it is important to contain any feelings that are at all negative. Avoid engaging in gossip this month. What you say will tend to be repeated in the wrong context, putting you in the hot seat. It could even cost you your promotion. Keep your horoscope allies and friends close to you to garner the luck of helpful people in your life.

BUSINESS – *Caught in the Crossfire*

Business benefits from new strategies and directions this month, but however certain you feel that you have all the answers, there is always benefit to be gained from picking the brains of others. Allow some of your generals in the company to get more involved in pitching ideas. Be encouraging. This could be a good time to branch out into something new.

Take on a strong leadership role this month. Concentrate on those who work with you. Make your employees feel that they have a stake in the company. This will increase productivity and there will be newfound enthusiasm at the workplace. This is also a good month to expand your network. Make an effort to socialize at cocktails and other such affairs, you could meet someone inspiring and valuable.

LOVE & RELATIONSHIPS – *Socialite Month*

Catching up with old friends is the best way to meet new people. Make it a point to attend social events you get invited to. Take the initiative to throw a few parties yourself. When it comes to love, this is your lucky month, because you have blessings from heaven and your union luck is strong. Others find you fascinating to be around. When you meet new people, don't try too hard to impress. Others will be most impressed if you come across real. Avoid name-dropping; it is as annoying as it is ineffective this month. If you are married you can look forward to a stable family life with little disruption from work pressure. You're able to breathe and truly enjoy your spouse and kids. If you're been missing the excitement in your marriage, plan a trip away or even a romantic night on the town. Trying a bit harder will make all the difference.

EDUCATION – *Teacher's Pet*

This is a good time to get closer to your teachers, especially if you are ambitious in your academic career. Finding the right mentor will make all the difference this month. If you have any questions or issues you want to raise, try discussing them with your parents. Tapping the brains of someone older will cause everything to click for you much more quickly.

10TH MONTH
Nov 7th - Dec 6th 2010

BETTER TO STAY LOW KEY

The five yellow this month brings misfortune and illness, and overall quite an unfortunate month. You are likely to run up against some hard luck; but treat any difficulties you meet up with as problems you have to solve. If you look at them that way, you'll find the solution in no time. But stressing out won't solve anything and will only make you ill. Avoid taking risks this month, especially with your money. You should also take care when it comes to rough or contact sports. Wear metal or the color white to counter this month's energies.

WORK & CAREER – *Challenging Scenario*

Work is definitely not going to be a walk in the park this month. There are many challenges to face. These will not just be in the form of completing projects on time or doing your job well. Personalities clash and someone at work could be making your life miserable. Do not allow them to get you down. If ignoring them doesn't do the trick, try showing your wrathful side once in a while. Being the nice guy all the time doesn't always work. Protect yourself and your interests at work by maintaining good relations with your superiors. You may have your tiffs with co-workers who see themselves in competition with you, but don't cross the line with insubordination. If you think you are being treated unfairly, wait and see if things change next month.

BUSINESS — *Obstacles Crop Up*

This is a strategically bad month to make new investments. Conserve your cash and avoid taking too many risks. Avoid important meetings; leave this till another time. There may be a few financial ups and downs to face this month. Some may be worrying, but don't let yourself get overly worked up because things will work out in the end. Avoid losing too much money by wearing amulets in gold. You can wear the **Lock Coin,** or carry a **golden double horned rhinoceros.** The **mystic knot** also has protective properties that will benefit you this month.

LOVE & RELATIONSHIPS — *Go Easy*

You face hidden tension in your relationships this month. Big fights may sprout up from innocent squabbles. Don't let jealousy get the better of you. Accusing your partner of flirting with other people will only drive the two of you apart. If you are serious about keeping your relationship, don't push each other to a corner. Give each other some space. Pour your energies

into other things if your love life isn't working out.
You may be feeling emotionally vulnerable, but talking
things over repeatedly will only drain you more. Steer
the conversation to lighter topics if you find yourself
focusing on problems that are getting you down.

EDUCATION – *Risk of Injury*

Be more careful in sports and physical activities this
month. There is risk of accidents and injury. Do not
overdo things or you could get a muscle or ligament
strain. Wear a **5 Element Pagoda** charm made of gold
or metal on you to protect against the negative stars in
your chart this month. In your school work, if you're
just feeling too tired, get some sleep before trying to
complete assignments. Chances are you have a lot on
your mind and are not in the best of moods when it
comes to studying or revising.

HOME & FAMILY – *Noisy At Home*

Quarrels and misunderstandings make life very
confrontational all round. Concentrate on staying calm
and taking things easy. Avoid disputes by steering clear
of contentious subject matters in conversation. Make
it a point to be nice. It is better to be overly nice than
nasty. Place an urn of **still yin water** in the NE sector
of your living room, and make sure there is no loud
activity in this part of the house this month. Switch
TVs and radios off in this part of the house.

11TH MONTH
Dec 7th - Jan 5th 2011

GOOD MONTH FOR A HOLIDAY

Disharmony at home causes distractions so it may be better to go on holiday. Romance is in the air and the married Ox enjoys a good month. In-laws and extended family however may get on your nerves. On the whole a pleasant time, but not one for focusing on anything too serious. This is good time for poets and dreamers. Creativity gets boosted so if your line of work involves lots of original thought, you could find yourself particularly prolific this month. There is good fortune for writers, actors and those in the media business. The student Ox also benefits from the chi energies of the month.

WORK & CAREER – *Taking Time Off*

Relationship luck is particularly good. Make the most of this by cultivating a good rapport with your boss. Your mind is relaxed and you are in a happy mood. Mixing with others causes your good nature to rub off and their countenance will mirror yours. People want to be your friend and help you. Make the most of their generous nature while it lasts. While you may be in relaxed mode, watch you don't get lazy, or the goodwill you create through your charm could be negated pretty quick.

BUSINESS – *In Your Prime*

A good time to develop friendships with business associates. You find yourself having great affinity with just about everyone. People take an instant liking to you and you have the knack of saying just the right thing at the right time. When pitching an idea, others respond positively. You make a good spokesperson this month as you can outtalk just about anybody. Make use of this talent by working doubly hard and you could reap double the rewards.

LOVE & RELATIONSHIPS – *Exciting*

This is an exciting time when it comes to love! You have an enthusiastic air about you that is quite infectious. Others enjoy your company and if you have someone special in mind, this is the right time to make the big moves! At parties you attract plenty of attention. You make a charismatic fixture at any soiree and will find yourself on all the must-be-on guest lists. When playing the dating game however, keep things open and honest. If you don't, it will be difficult for any relationship you strike up now to last into the longer term.

EDUCATION – *Becoming a Star!*

Scholars and students do well in their work and

exams this month. If you're prepared to study hard, you won't find it a problem getting the grades. The stars are definitely on your side. Boost study luck by placing a **Chi Lin with the 4 Scholastic Objects** in the NE of your study room or bedroom When education luck is good is when you should enhance it. You are hungry for knowledge and with the right teacher, you could go really far this month.

HOME & FAMILY – *Let the Money Flow*

This is a good time for charity work. If you have spare cash, think about giving some of it away to those who need it more than you. Your thoughts for now will lie not with material wealth and assets. You're more concerned with the spiritual aspects in life. If splurging on yourself makes you happy, go ahead and buy something. But you'll find that spending the money on others will be so much more fulfilling right now.

HEALTH & FITNESS – *Sleep Well*

You would feel both mentally and physically stronger if you find the time to get enough sleep each day. Ox doing too much could have nervous energy to burn. Make time to head to the gym or sports club to engage in an hour's hard core exercise at least three times a week. Try to work up a sweat. If you focus on your fitness, you'll be feeling fine as a fiddle in no time.

12TH MONTH
Jan 6th - Feb 3rd 2011

WATCH OUT FOR GOSSIP

There is severe bad luck caused by quarrels this month. You may find yourself a victim of gossip, which can be hurtful at the trivial level or libel at the more serious level. You're in a fighting mood and if someone else picks a fight, you are unlikely to back down. However, that may be just the thing you should do. You don't have the luck to "win" arguments this month. You may even face court cases and litigation. Keep the NE sector quiet, and even unoccupied if you can help it. You also need the Fire Sword to counter backstabbing. Could be a stressful month. Surround yourself with friends and people who make you feel better about yourself. Your ego could use a boost right now.

WORK & CAREER – *Transforming Your Attitude*

You can cover plenty of ground at work this month. Try not to let your inner demons sabotage your efforts to make a good impression. There are a multitude of things to keep you on your toes and if your usual response to stress is explosive, you'll need to learn to control your rage. If there is something really bothering you, talk to someone about it. But better to turn to family or friends than collagues from the office. You need someone removed from the whole situation to advise you. Shift your focus from things that get your goat up to things that please you. This has the ability shift your attitude as well, something you could definitely use right now.

BUSINESS – *Avoid Being Hardnosed*

While you may be feeling ambitious, avoid being hardnosed when doing business. Such self-serving behavior will only trip you up. Your argumentative nature will make it hard for you to engage in meaningful and civil discussion, particularly over issues you are passionate about. Although you may have big plans you can't wait to put in action, don't be impatient. Wait it out and aim to get things started only next month. Channel your energy into working alone now, rather than attempting to network too much this month.

LOVE & RELATIONSHIPS – *Apologize!*

Your usual smooth talking may come out wrong this month. Be prepared to do some explaining, and apologize whether you're in the wrong or not. You may not feel like molly coddling anyone right now, but in the interest of peace, you may have no choice. Work on your personal charm; you have it in you but your ego may not let you draw it out. A good way to smooth out a big quarrel is to buy your better half a gift. It needn't be expensive; it's the thought that counts.

HOME & FAMILY – *Create Harmony*

Your relationships with family members face a rocky patch this month. You find yourself irritable with a short fuse, and don't suffer fools gladly. Whenever you feel like blowing your top, bite your tongue because saying the wrong thing now could have some longer term and quite damaging consequences. Display the **Makara Dragon** in the living room to promote greater harmony among at home, and learn to chill out.

EDUCATION – *Don't take Shortcuts*

If you catch yourself taking short cuts in your work, stop yourself in your tracks. Set yourself an aim each day of what you want to accomplish. It is better right now for you to work alone than with others. Your argumentative nature will only slow you down if you work in a group. Make time for relaxation, but preferably in a form of exercise rather than hanging out in a mall.

Display the Makara Dragon in the living room to promote a more harmonious home life. Important for the Ox.

Part 4
Updating House Feng Shui

To maintain good feng shui in your home and to ensure a smooth transition into the new year, you need to add a **time dimension** to your use of feng shui. This means making some vital changes to the placement of decorative objects, making alterations to the way furniture is arranged in the public areas of your home and sometimes even making adjustments to room usage.

Making changes to accommodate the new annual chi is important to maintain a balance of good energy in the home. This is what will help residents enjoy a better year, as you are then protected against getting hit by nasty surprises and misfortune happenings.

The changes in energy each new year is something not many people are aware of, as a result of which, even when a home has been very well designed according to feng shui principles, when no effort is made to accommodate yearly changes of energy, sometimes bad luck descends unexpectedly, causing sudden problems to descend on the family; and often, misfortune brought by afflictive flying stars can be quite severe, serious enough to cause a high degree of stress and tribulations.

When unlucky energy inadvertently flies into the part of your home where your **main door** is located, or where your **bedroom** is sited, you and often your family as well risk being hit by some kind of misfortune. This may be a sudden illness, an unexpected accident or loss, a court case or a significant reversal of fortune that brings hardship. It is advisable to anticipate this kind of problem, address it and install remedies and cures. This is the best way to practice feng shui with great effectiveness.

The location and severity of feng shui afflictions that bring bad luck to residents are revealed by annual flying stars. These are numbers that move around a specially constructed feng shui chart based on an ancient formula that maps out the changing chi movements of each new year. These changes alter the way the luck of any home plays out in any given year. It is part of the time aspect of feng shui and is something that should be incorporated into an annual renewal of chi program for the home. Attending to this ensures that the energy of abodes stay fresh and vigorous.

Yearly Feng Shui Afflictions

Annual afflictions bring negative luck, causing misfortune, accidents, loss and a variety of ills to manifest. This part of the book explains the severity and location of the different afflictions in the Year of the Tiger. Once you know what and where the afflictions are, it is not difficult to deal with them using element cures and other traditional feng shui methods.

> It is important to subdue annual feng shui afflictions because these have the potential to create havoc in your life.

Misfortune can come in a variety of ways. Sometimes they manifest as severe illness or they can cause loss of wealth, loss of good name or loss of a loved one. It is not difficult to control feng shui afflictions and doing so helps prevent bad luck from occurring, so everyone should take the trouble to do so.

In the past, this aspect of feng shui practice was simply ignored by modern day practitioners, leaving many vulnerable to reversals of fortune, but in recent years, awareness of time dimension feng shui has increased substantially. Master practitioners of feng shui in Asia and around the world now go to great lengths to study, analyze and deal with time related feng shui afflictions at the start of each New Year.

The cut-off date when energy patterns change occurs around February 4th, which is regarded as the first day of Spring – in Chinese known as the *lap chun*. This is not to be confused with the lunar New Year date which is determined by the Chinese lunar calendar. The Chinese use their solar calendar (known as the *Hsia Calendar*) to track feng shui energy changes. The monthly change of energy patterns in Part 3 of the book, for instance, uses the Hsia calendar to determine the dates when each month starts.

The feng shui chart of any year is usually depicted in a 9 x 9 sector Lo Shu square with a number in each grid. These numbers are determined by the ruling or center number which in 2010 is 8. Once the center number is known, the rest of the numbers in the different grids of the Lo Shu square can be determined.

2010 Annual Feng Shui Chart

SE	S	SW
7	3	5
E 6	8	1 W
2	4	9
NE	N	NW

The numbers in this chart change or "fly" from year to year, reflecting changes in energy in the different direction sectors. Each of the numbers in the different compass locations reveals the quality of energy ruling that location in 2010.

The numbers 1 through 9 in each of the nine grids of the Lo Shu Square offer insights into the way the pattern of luck has moved in any built-up structure or building. This investigation precedes the updating of feng shui. In addition to afflictions, the chart also reveals the good luck sectors - i.e. those parts of your house that enjoy the most auspicious luck during the year.

If the lucky numbers fly into the sector that houses your main door or bedroom, or into any part of the home where you spend a considerable amount of time, the good energy of that location will shower you with good fortune.

Sometimes the feng shui of your bedroom can be so good it can override any kind of low energy you may be suffering from your horoscope for the year.

When auspicious numbers enter into the location of your animal sign, it will benefit you for that year. Hence understanding the annual chart enables you to subdue bad luck and bad feng shui; and to enhance good luck and good feng shui.

When feng shui afflictions of your living and work spaces are treated with feng shui cures, and the lucky sectors are activated with auspicious decorative objects or celestial creatures, your luck for the year is sure to instantly improve.

You can overcome obstacles to success more effectively, and make better decisions by tracking your luck through each month of the year. Timing plays a crucial role and when armed with prior knowledge of good and bad months, you are certain to have a positive competitive edge.

Updating your feng shui brings powerful benefits as you will know exactly how protect against sudden/ major changes of fortunes. Those unprotected are vulnerable not only to annual afflictions but also to monthly ill winds that might be blowing your way. It is so important then to know about good and bad months.

Misfortune usually comes suddenly, descending on you when least expected. It can come as illness, or manifest as court action, or worse, as some kind of personal loss. Misfortune can hit at anytime. Don't think that bad things do not happen to good people because they do. Since it requires so little effort to guard against and bad feng shui, it seems foolish not to do so.

Luck of Different Parts of the Home

The annual feng shui chart reveals the luck of every part of the house categorized into compass sectors based on their respective locations. So every compass corner of the home must be investigated. Each sector has a number from 1 through 9, and this comprises eight outer sectors plus the center. In 2010, the center sector ruling number is 8, and this allows the numbers of the outer 8 sectors to be identified.

These numbers enable a knowledgeable feng shui practitioner to instantly be able to identify afflicted sectors. These are the parts of the house where cures and remedies need to be put into place because doing so brings protection to the whole house!

In the same way, the luckiest sectors can also be ascertained and then activated to manifest good luck. When individual sectors get enhanced, the improved chi energy spreads to the rest of the house. It is therefore necessary to study the feng shui chart for 2010, then superimpose it onto the layout sketches of your home, using a good compass to anchor the directions.

Please always remember to use a good compass to determine the compass sectors of your home.

Familiarize yourself with the chart of 2010 and systematically list down the afflictions that are particularly harmful for your house. Remember that when bad luck numbers occur in rooms that you or your family use often, that is when placing the correct remedies and cures take on some urgency. If the bad luck numbers fall into store rooms, toilets, kitchens or to parts of house that make up missing corners, then the misfortune-bringing numbers should have little negative effect. When these bad luck numbers come into your bedroom, or afflict important doors and areas of the home (such as the dining area and family area) then once again, remedies become very important.

The same analogy applies to good luck stars. When these fly into important and heavy traffic rooms, the auspicious luck gets activated, and they then bring benefits to residents. When they enter into small rooms like store rooms or tight little alcoves, their good effect does not benefit the household as much.

Activating Good Star Numbers

You need to remember that in Flying Star feng shui, good and bad luck numbers need to be activated either by placing an object that symbolizes a producing element (such as Water element producing Wood element in a Wood sector like East or SE) or with an auspicious decorative item. Here, knowing what **celestial creature** to display and what **element** is favorable for the year will help you to vastly improve your home feng shui.

Other ways to activate or energize good numbers is to increase the level of yang energy in the corners benefiting from the year's good fortune numbers. Thus using bright lights and increasing sound levels in the center of the house in 2010, should benefit the household greatly. This is because the center plays host to the auspicious 8 and activating it is sure to bring benefits.

In 2010, the center of the house should be energized by the presence of **multiple crystal balls** – eight is an excellent number. This strengthens the earth element of the center and since 8 is itself an Earth element number, and considering that the Earth element symbolizes wealth in 2010, enhancing Earth energy is excellent indeed.

Crystal balls of any kind will be very beneficial for the center of the home in 2010. The large **Tara Crystal Ball** which we brought out last year to energize 8 in the SE then was a great success for many people and for those who want to use these again this year, just move it to the center of the room. Make sure you twirl it daily because this activates the positive effects of crystal ball. As the ball contains the praises to the Goddess Tara, twirling the ball activates its wish fulfilling aspect.

There is also another crystal ball which contains the powerful six syllable *Om Mani Padme Hum* mantra in Tibetan. For those wanting to create an aura of blessings in the home you can also place this **Om Mani Crystal Ball** in the center of the home, or on the coffee table in the living room. A golden 8 embedded inside the crystal ball activates the power of 8.

We have also designed a beautiful **Crystal 8** with real gold flakes embedded within to be placed in the center of the home. This will add significantly to the enhancement of the Earth element which will be so beneficial in 2010. Another powerful enhancer which can be placed in the center of the home to activate the auspicious 8 is the **Victory Banner Windchime**.

Victory Banner windchimes placed in the center of the home will activate the power of the lucky 8.

Feng Shui Chart of 2010

The feng shui chart of 2010 is created by placing
the ruling number of the year in the center. We have
already taken note that the ruling number of the year
is 8, and considering we are currently in the Period of
8, this makes the number 8 extremely significant and
very lucky indeed.

2010 Year of the Golden Tiger

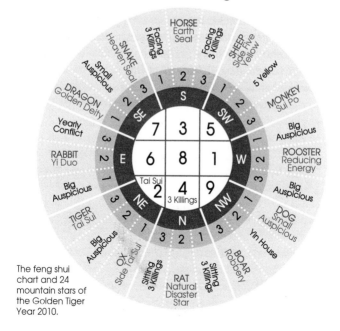

The feng shui
chart and 24
mountain stars of
the Golden Tiger
Year 2010.

Activating the 8 in the center brings amazing good fortune and this is why we are strongly recommending the crystal 8 with gold for the center of the house! Those whose Kua number or Lo Shu number is 8 can expect the year to go well for them, as this is also the period of 8.

This also includes women whose Kua number is 5. This is because Kua number 5 transforms to 8 for women. Just make sure you make an effort to activate the 8 in the center of the house.

You can check the Lo Shu and Kua numbers of your loved ones and friends from the resource tables contained in our *Feng Shui Diary 2010*. The feng shui chart of the year can be used to study the feng shui of any building, but you must use a compass to get your bearings and to anchor the directions of the different rooms of your house or office. Then systematically investigate the luck of every sector.

Luck Stars of the 24 Mountains

In addition to numbers of the chart, we study the influences of the stars that fly into the 24 mountain directions of the compass. These "stars" do not carry the same weighting in terms of their strength and luck -bringing potential, but they add important nuances to annual chart readings, and are extracted from the Almanac. Incorporating the influence of the stars adds depth to a reading of the year's feng shui energy for each of the twelve signs.

Together, the stars and numbers reveal accurate things about the year, and when we add the influence of the year's elements, readings for each animal sign become very potent and exciting. This assists you to get the best from the year. The seamless merging of Chinese Zodiac Astrology with feng shui comprises the core strength and great value of our little astrology books, which we take great joy and pride in researching and writing every year.

This is the seventh year of our *Fortune & Feng Shui* list. Each year we delve a little deeper into all that influences the fortune and luck of the 12 animal signs, and the recommendations contained herein take account of these influences. Please use the analysis in this section to move from sector to sector and from room to room in your home, systematically installing feng shui remedies affected by bad chi energy. Place powerful decorative energizers and protective images to create and safeguard good luck.

ILLNESS STAR 2
Hits the Northeast in 2010

SE	S	SW
7	3	5
6	8	1
2	4	9
NE	N	NW

E (left side) · W (right side)

This is the Illness Star which flies to NE in 2010. The "star" brings propensity to getting sick for those whose bedroom or door is located in the NE sector of the home.

The illness star 2 flies to the NE in 2010. This is an Earth element sector and since the illness star 2 is an Earth element number, it makes the illness affliction extremely strong in the Year of the Tiger.

Earth flying into Earth suggests that those residing in the NE of their homes, or having an office or a front door in the NE, tend to be vulnerable to getting sick.

Unless the illness-bringing energy in this part of buildings (homes and offices) is strongly suppressed, people residing or working in that part of the building are likely to develop physical ailments. And since the illness star is strong this year, it is harder to control.

The two animal signs affected by the illness star are the Tiger and Ox, who are Wood and Earth respectively. The Tiger's Wood is an effective foil to the Earth star of illness, but for the Ox, the illness star is likely to pose a serious health threat. It is also a good idea not to spend too much time in the NE part of your living room or home.

If your bedroom is located in the NE of your house, make sure suitable remedies are placed to suppress illness vibes. When the main door of the house is located in the NE, the constant opening and closing of the door is sure to activate the illness-bringing star. It is advisable to try and use another door located in another sector. If this is not possible, then try exhausting the Earth energy here. Remove all Earth element items such as crystals, porcelain vases or stone objects. Also keep lights here dim to reduce Fire element energy. This is because Fire element strengthens Earth element.

Cures for the Illness Star of 2010

There are excellent remedies that can be used to suppress the illness star. In 2010, a **Tiger/Dragon Wu Lou** would be especially effective. Another excellent cure is the **Antakarana Symbol** which is powerful enough to suppress the strong illness star this year, especially when it is made of metal. Brass is especially good as Metal exhausts the Earth energy of the illness star. The symbol itself is a powerful symbol of healing and has a three dimensional effect that cuts directly into harmful negative energy. Get this symbol and place under the bed if your bed is located in the NE of your bedroom, or if your bedroom itself is in the NE. Those born in the years of the Ox and Tiger are strongly advised to sleep with the symbol of the Antakarana under their pillows or wear the Antakarana ring preferably made in yellow gold. Similar cures also benefit those born in the years of the Dog and the Horse, and those born in the years of the Rooster and the Snake. The energies emitted by the powerful Antakarana symbols will effectively keep sickness at bay.

The healing symbol of Antahkarana.

LITIGATION STAR 3
Hits the South in 2010

SE	S	SW
7	3	5
6	8	1
2	4	9
NE	N	NW

(E on left side, W on right side)

This is the unlucky 3 Star which brings court cases & quarrels. It flies to the South in 2010, affecting all of you whose room or office is located in the South. Use red or Fire energy to suppress.

The quarrelsome star 3, which brings the aggravating energy of litigation and court cases flies to the South of homes and offices in 2010. This star brings an air of hostility and creates a variety of problems associated with arguments, fights and misunderstandings to everyone directly hit by it. In extreme cases, when this Wood element star is enhanced, the quarrelling can lead to court cases and even violence for residents spending time in the South.

The number 3 star can cause a host of interpersonal strife to flare up even between the closest of allies, friends and loved ones. It causes tempers to fray and usually manifests in a great deal of impatience. Fortunately for anyone having a bedroom in the South, the quarrelsome star 3 is less strong this year because its intrinsic Wood element is exhausted by the Fire energy of the South.

The 3 Star is a Wood star and the traditional way of overcoming this is to exhaust it with Fire energy. Anything that suggests Fire is an excellent cure, so all kinds of lights and the color red are suitable. Hence because the South is so strongly associated with Fire energy, the sector itself has its own in-built remedy!

Earth Seal in the South

A good indication for the South location (and for those born in the year of the Horse) in 2010 is that the sector benefits from the presence of the **Earth Seal** brought by the luck star of the 24 mountains. This brings good fortune to those residing in this part of the house, especially if you take action to enhance this energy with Earth element activators such as solid crystal or glass globes.

Houses that face South should place the **Fire Sword** here as a safeguard against being hauled into court or getting involved in a tiresome legal battle perhaps left over from past years. If you are already involved in a prolonged battle with someone or some company, the number 3 star will hurt you if you have a bedroom in the South or if your house is facing South.

If this is the case with you, use **strong bright lights** to help overcome it. A dramatic remedy which brings some relief from aggravation is simply to paint the South part of the house a bright red – perhaps a wall or door if this is the front part of the home.

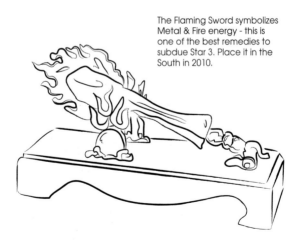

The Flaming Sword symbolizes Metal & Fire energy - this is one of the best remedies to subdue Star 3. Place it in the South in 2010.

MISFORTUNE STAR 5
Hits the Southwest in 2010

SE	S	SW
7	3	5
6	8	1
2	4	9
NE	N	NW

The Five Yellow Star, flies to the SW hurting the matriarchal energy of every home. This is a serious affliction which must be suppressed with the 5 element pagoda with "Hum" empowering syllable.

The Five Yellow star, also known as the *wu wang*, flies to the SW in 2010, making it a very serious affliction this year. This is a star to be feared as it brings aggravations, misfortunes and most of all in 2010, a big weakness to the Matriarch of the family.

This is because SW is usually associated with the mother energy of any home. And in feng shui, when the matriarchal energy gets afflicted, it usually has a strong impact on the rest of the family as well. This is because the SW is the source of the family's nurturing chi.

As we are currently in the period of 8, the SW/NE directional axis exerts a great deal of strong chi for any home and when the energy of this axis brings misfortune, it must be firmly subdued. In 2010 this axis direction appears to be powerfully afflicted, with the Five Yellow in the SW and 2 in the NE.

> The *wu wang* is very dangerous in normal years, but in 2010, it is extremely strong as it is an earth star flying into an earth sector. Likewise the illness star 2 in the NE is also strong! The *wu wang* thus gets strengthened, as a result of which, it can create havoc for mothers and also for other older women of the household.

Those having their bedroom in the SW will also feel its negative impact, and when a house faces SW, the *wu wang* can bring bad luck which affects the entire household. If there is a door in the SW that you frequently use, the *wu wang* gets activated, and this further compounds its strength. It is advisable to use another door if possible. The opening and closing of doors activates the energy around it.

Everyone should suppress the pernicious effects of this number 5 star – otherwise its negative influence can spread to other parts of the house. It must be strongly curbed with metallic and remedies. These should be prominently placed, on a table or sideboard in the SW of the house and office as well as in the SW of afflicted bedrooms and living rooms.

Cures for the Wu Wang

For 2010, we recommend three powerful cures for this affliction. These should be used together for fast and powerful results.

1) **Five Element Pagoda with Ten Powerful Mantras**

This year, this traditional remedy comes with a larger base and the powerful mantras are stamped all round the base of the pagoda. This version of the five element pagoda is recommended for use in larger rooms and is best when placed above ground, preferably on a table. The mantras on the pagoda transform it into a powerful object which should be respected, so place it on a table.

The Five Element Pagoda with Ten Powerful Mantras is one of the most effective cures for the *wu wang*.

2) The **Five Element Big Bell**
This cure is best when 12 inches high The bell is
divided into 5 horizontal sections, each one signifying
the 5 elements. The bell also has powerful mantras
embossed on its outside. The remedy comes from
striking of the bell. Here, the sound of metal struck on
metal is what will suppress the negative influences of
the Five Yellow. Strike the bell at least once a day, and
more often if residents are going through a hard time.
The sound of the bell with the resonance of the mantras
is very powerful for dispelling bad vibes. All misfortune
luck gets alleviated instantly. This is the most powerful
cure against the five yellow. If you prefer, you can use
the ringing bell instead, and the way to suppress the *wu
wang* is to ring this bell each day.

3) **Double Circle Pendant**
If you want to ensure continuous suppression of any
ongoing misfortune luck or if you or your family are
going through tough times associated with broken
relationships and loss of income (such as losing your
job) it is beneficial for family members to wear the
Double Circle pendant. This will activate powerful
Metal energy to exhaust the effects of the *wu wang*.
Better yet if the pendant has multiple circles and in
the center there is a square design. This indicates the
wu wang is kept under control.

Please note that unless suppressed, the *wu wang* brings severe illness, accidents and loss that occur in many aspects of life. It is the catalyst for bringing all kinds of misfortune. It can cause your life to suddenly collapse around you. When you read about tragedies striking a family, you can be sure that the five yellow is somehow responsible, either because it afflicts the main door or the room the person occupies. Sometimes, just facing the *wu wang* direction can bring some kind of bad luck.

If your main door, bedroom or office desk is afflicted by the wu wang, the affliction must be dealt with before the 4th February 2010. Do not be careless or forget about it as bad luck can manifest quickly. When it does it might be too late to do something about it. Prevention is better than cure, so do not wait until it is too late.

Those living in SW facing houses should take note of the months when you need to be extra careful of the five yellow. We stress this because it is a serious feng shui affliction in 2010. As a person born in the Ox year you must **be extra careful in the month of November** as this is the month when the Five Yellow also flies into your month chart. This is when you are subjected to a double whammy of bad luck so do be careful.

Misfortunes caused by the Five Yellow in 2010 can be severe business loss or threatening terminal illness.

Houses that face the SW require one or all three of the remedies suggested. This is because houses that face SW are sitting NE which is being hit by the illness star. Metal energy works well here at both the front and back of the house.

If you reside in a room located in the SW, your cures should be inside your room. Make sure that the cures are in place from February 4th, the start of the Chinese solar year. While remedies used in previous years can be recycled after they have been cleansed with salt, it is better to retire them by throwing them into the sea or a fast moving river. It is always better to use new products with fresh new energy. New remedies are better for suppressing feng shui afflictions, as the energy of new objects are more vigorous and thus more effective.

Ox people belong to the Earth element, so the *wu wang*'s Earth element brings competitive pressures into their life. This is one of the effects of the *wu wang* affliction on the Ox – more people tend to want to compete with you or manifest envy and jealousy. Also, in 2010, the element of Earth stands for wealth luck that is in danger of declining in value due to the lack of water during the year. To be safeguarded from these two kinds of misfortunes, Ox must try not to be afflicted by this powerful misfortune star.

Observe the "NO RENOVATION RULE" for the Southwest in 2010

It is extremely harmful if you were to undertake any kind of knocking, banging or digging in the SW in 2010. This will especially hurt the mother of the household. So do observe the "No Renovation" rule for the SW during 2010. Any kind of demolition work poses serious danger. Misfortunes are sure to manifest.

It is especially dangerous to drill floors, knock down walls, dig holes in the ground, engage in any kind of destructive work or make excessive banging kind of noise. Any of these activities have the effect of activating the wu wang which in turn is sure to trigger very severe misfortune luck to suddenly manifest. The way to safeguard against this is to keep the SW location of the home very quiet in 2010.

If you really have to undertake renovations in your house and it encroaches into the SW sector, make sure your cures are in place **and** make very sure the renovation does not start or end in the SW. No one should be staying in the SW sector when renovations are going on. If you are adding to the SW however, and not disturbing the space with banging and digging, then that kind of renovation is acceptable; and can even be auspicious. But as long as you are demolishing or digging the earth/floor, it is advisable to postpone whatever you may be planning for the sector.

ROBBERY STAR 7
Strikes the Southeast in 2010

SE	S	SW
7	3	5
6	8	1
2	4	9
NE	N	NW

The Robbery Star brings violence & turmoil in your life. At its worse, the 7 brings armed robbery that can cause fatal results. Protect against it with the Blue Rhino & Elephant.

This is a very unwelcome affliction that is brought by the number 7. It is a number that causes political turmoil and sparks aggressive behavior that can become something serious very quickly. This is because it is the violent star. It brings out the worst in all who come under its influence or is afflicted by it.

In 2010, it flies to the SE where its presence creates dangerous situations for those residing here in the SE sector. This star number completely dominates the sector because being of the Metal Element, it easily controls the Wood Element of the SE. So the 7 is very lethal here.

The SE is the place of the eldest daughter so daughters should be especially careful. Anyone living in the SE should also be very careful as this star number brings danger of violence and burglary. It is advisable to try and avoid this sector.

> For 2010, because the Water element is so lacking during the year, the best remedy for the SE - for the whole house to be protected from the 7 star - is to display the **Blue Rhinoceros and Elephant Water Globe**. This will be a very powerful cure for the violent burglary star.

The good news is that in the year 2010 the *Luck Stars of the 24 Mountains* for the SE are extremely auspicious. Thus the *Star of the Golden Deity,* which brings heaven's blessings, benefits all those residing in the SE1 location. At the same time, the SE3 location is favored by the *Heavenly Seal* which also brings auspicious energy. This benefits anyone staying here.

These two powerful heavenly stars of the 24 mountains are an excellent buffer against the burglary star as it is sandwiched between two powerful stars. This helps residents of the SE overcome burglary woes in 2010.

In terms of feng shui, the best way to overcome the negative effect of 7 is to have a large water feature, as Water exhausts the vitality of 7.

Water is also auspicious for the SE where it strengthens the intrinsic Wood energy here. Those who already have a Water feature here such as a pond in the garden or an internal water feature in the living room will be happy to know that in addition to generating good fortune luck for the eldest daughter of the family, water here will suppress the Burglary Star and bring wonderful much needed water element energy for the year.

The Tai Sui Resides in the Northeast in 2010

The 2010 *Tai Sui* resides in the location of NE3 which is the home location of the crouching Tiger; however, despite occupying the den of the Tiger, this year's Tai Sui is not wrathful, and like the Tai Sui of the previous year, is not quick to anger even when disturbed or confronted. Nevertheless, to be on the safe side, it is advisable to keep the Tai Sui appeased and happy. The best way of doing this is to place the **Tai Sui plaque** with specially written Taoist talisman. This not only appeases the Tai Sui, it also successfully enlists the Tai Sui's help to attract prosperity and abundance.

The Tai Sui is in a side conflict with those born in the year of the Ox, due to your Ox location being in close proximity to the Tiger location. However the Ox is able to withstand the Tai Sui affliction as it is enjoying the 24 Mountain Star of Big Auspicious. Nevertheless, it is advisable to use the **Tai Sui amulet** to be safeguarded from this affliction.

The Effect of the Tai Sui Affliction

The Chinese who believe in feng shui take the affliction of the Tai Sui very seriously as emphasized in the *Treatise on Harmonizing Times and Distinguishing Directions* compiled under the patronage of the Qianlong Emperor during his reign in the mid Eighteenth century. The Emperor placed great importance on the astrological influences on the luck of the dynasty. He stressed particularly on the correct ways for selecting times and aligning houses and went to great lengths to ensure that all knowledge on these matters were properly catalogued.

The Treatise confirms that the astrology of the Tai Sui has been recognized since mid century BCE (for over 2000 years) and states that the locations where the Tai Sui resides and where the Tai Sui has just vacated are lucky locations. So note that in 2010, the locations of NE1 and NE3 are lucky. Those having their rooms in these two locations will enjoy the patronage and protection of the Tai Sui in 2010.

The Treatise explains that it is unlucky to reside in the location where the Tai Sui is progressing towards i.e. clockwise on the astrology compass and in 2010, this means the East 2 location; it is unlucky to directly confront the Tai Sui's residence. It is unlucky to 'face' the Tai Sui because this is deemed rude, so the advice for 2010 is not to directly face NE3 direction. Actually doing so also causes you to directly confront the Tiger and this is definitely not advisable.

So for 2010 you must remember not to face NE3 even if this is your most favored direction under Eight Mansions Feng Shui. When you face the Tai Sui, nothing you do will go smoothly as obstacles surface unexpectedly and friends turn into adversaries. Be careful of this facing direction taboo in 2010 if you don't want your good fortune to get blocked by the Tai Sui. **Do not face the NE3 direction.**

Important Reminder

An important reminder for 2010 is to not disturb the place of the Tai Sui which means the NE3 location should not be renovated this year. Refrain from drilling, digging, banging and knocking down walls or digging holes in the ground. Those starting renovations in 2010 to change to a Period 8 house are advised not to start or end their renovations in NE3 and to avoid starting or ending their renovations in November when the direction of the Tai Sui is afflicted by misfortune star of *wu wang*.

Do not start or
end renovations
in the NE this year.

It is very beneficial to place the beautiful **Pi Yao** in the NE as this celestial chimera is incredibly auspicious. For getting on the good side of the Tai Sui they are also effective. They also bring exceptional good fortune into the home. Get them in jade or any earth colour to enhance their power in a year when Wood chi brings wealth and Earth chi brings productive resources.

The Three Killings
Flies to the North in 2010

In 2010 the North of every building is afflicted by the three killings. This feng shui aggravation affects only the primary directions, but that means its bad effects are felt over a larger area of the house – 90 degrees!

This affliction brings three severe misfortunes associated with loss, grief and sadness. Its location each year is charted according to the animal sign that rules the year. Thus it flies to the North in 2010 because the Tiger belongs to the Triangle of Affinity made up of the Tiger, Dog and Horse, and of these three animal signs it is the Horse which occupies a cardinal direction (South). The Three Killings is thus in the North, the direction that is directly opposite the Horse.

The Three Killings cause three kinds of loss, the loss of one's good reputation, the loss of a loved one and the loss of wealth. When you suffer a sudden reversal of fortune, it is usually due to being hit by the three killings. In 2010, the three killings reside in the North where it poses some danger to the middle sons of the family. Anyone occupying the North is very vulnerable to being hit by the three killings.

Cures for the Three Killings

In terms of cures, we recommend the three divine guardians comprising the Chi Lin, the Fu Dog and the Pi Yao. We have been using these celestial protectors with great success for several years now and can continue using them for 2010. It is however advisable to bring in newly minted ones to ensure their energy is fresh and there is strong vigor and vitality.

The three guardians are a great favorite with the Chinese and they create a powerful and invisible shield of protective energy that prevents the Three Killings from passing into the home or office. It is a good idea to keep all North sector doors and windows closed during

The Three Divine Guardians can be used to control the Three Killings affliction in the North in 2010.

the afternoon hours as this is an effective way of preventing the energy of the Three Killings from entering. Another powerful set of cures to overpower the Three Killings in the Year of the Tiger are the three deities each sitting on a Tiger and therefore symbolizing their dominance over this powerful beast. Deities that sit on the Tiger are usually also wealth-bringing Gods. The most effective is to line up the Wealth God sitting on a Tiger (Tsai Shen Yeh), the Eight Immortal sitting on a Tiger and one of the 18 Arhats sitting on a Tiger. If you prefer, you can also display just one of them.

The symbolism of these three powerful Deities cannot be matched and their presence in the home is also an effective way of avoiding all the difficult luck brought by the Tiger in 2010.

The Wealth God sitting on a Tiger symbolizes his dominance over the animal and displaying his image in the home helps you bring the fierce energies of the Tiger Year under control.

THE LUCKY STAR 4 bringing
Romance & Study Luck to the North

SE	S	SW
7	3	5
6	8	1
2	4	9
NE	N	NW

(E on left side, W on right side)

Lucky Star 4 flies North bringing love & romance this part of houses in 2010. The star 4 is also beneficial for anyone engaged in writing, study and work.

The North comes out of a challenging year to play host to the romance-bringing star in 2010. Last year, the North had been afflicted by the *wu wang*, but this year, this is the location which attracts love and marriage opportunities and developments of the heart brought by the peach blossom vibes here. This luck is considered good for singles and unmarried people but is viewed with suspicion for those who are already married.

Peach blossom luck is usually linked to temptations of the heart and to unfaithful behavior for the older married. As such, this is not a star favored by those already married. So if your room is in the North part of the house and you are already married, it is not a bad idea to symbolically suppress it with **bright lights** or Fire element energy. This should prevent either husband or wife succumbing to temptation coming their way. Placing an **amethyst geode** tied with red string and attached to the bed is a Taoist way of keeping the marriage stable, and spouses faithful.

Unmarried people who want to activate their marriage luck can do so with the presence of all the marriage symbols such as the **dragon and phoenix,** and the **double happiness character.** Here in the North, the romance star favors young men who are still single. Those of you keen on enhancing marriage luck should activate your peach blossom luck by placing a **Bejeweled Rat** in the North. However, do note that the Chinese usually do not favor romance blossoming in the year of the Tiger and they usually wait until the following year of the Rabbit before committing themselves in a new love relationship.

The double happiness symbol is ideal for attracting marriage luck. It should be worn or incorporated into house or room decor for best results.

Scholastic Luck

Those residing in the North will also enjoy the other influences brought by the same number 4 star which are related to scholastic and literary pursuits.

The number 4's literary side is strong, bringing academic luck to those residing in this part of the home. Those facing North also benefit from this powerful star of learning which is especially suitable for students and those sitting for examinations.

The direction North stands for career luck so this auspicious number is a very positive star here. The only problem will be that love can also be a distraction, so if you want to enhance the scholastic side of this star, you should place literary symbols here.

The number 4 benefits those engaged in writing and literary careers. Those employed in a writing career or in the media or are involved in any kind of academic pursuits benefit from staying in the North. Enhancing this part of the home is sure to bring benefits.

Feng shui energizers for the North are categorized into those benefiting the romance side and those wanting to activate the scholastic side. For love and romance, place **mandarin ducks** here or better yet hang a **love mirror** to reflect in the energies of the cosmic universe from outside. Meanwhile, those wanting to jumpstart their scholastic or literary pursuits should look for a good specimen of a **single-pointed quartz crystal** and then write a powerful wishfulfilling mantra on it. This is an excellent way of helping you to improve your concentration and your studies.

WHITE STAR 1 brings Triumphant Success to the West

SE	S	SW
7	3	5
6 (E)	8	1 (W)
2	4	9
NE	N	NW

The Victory Star is in the West. It is flanked by the 2 "Big Auspicious" stars of the 24 mountains. This makes the West sector extremely lucky in 2010 and those having rooms here can take advantage of this.

Those residing in rooms in the West will benefit from the white star of victory, the number 1 star, which brings triumph and success in 2010. This star number helps you to win in any competitive situation. The attainment of success is easier for you if you energize the number 1 star correctly and effectively.

The Victory Banner is a symbol of winning over the competition. Excellent for those in the running for a promotion.

In 2010, this star brings good fortune to **young women**, especially the youngest daughters of families and also the youngest women in any household. However, please note that the number 1 star in 2010 is not as vigorous as it was last year. There is definitely a relative reduction in energy. Anyone residing in this part of the house will benefit from having the **Victory Banner** placed here. It is important that this be made of brass metal to strengthen the metal element of this corner.

CELESTIAL STAR 6
Creates Windfall Luck in the East

SE	S	SW
7	3	5
E 6	8	1 W
2	4	9
NE	N	NW

The celestial 6 brings excellent news through the year. The number 6 stands for heavenly energy which unites with earth and mankind to create the trinity of Tien Ti Ren.

This is the number 6 white star associated with the powerful Trigram *Chien*, so its presence in the East creates synergy luck between father and eldest son. **When the bedroom of the family's eldest son is located in this sector of the house, he is certain to benefit very much from unexpected good fortune**, the kind that comes without warning, and is thus a welcome surprise. The 6 Star brings heaven's celestial blessings.

In Flying Star feng shui, the number 6 signifies everything to do with the management of economics and finances. At its peak, 6 stands for authority, influence and control over money, like being the Head of the Federal Reserve Board. When 6 appears in the East, it suggests economic power does well in the hands of a **young man**. This is also a military star which brings promotions and mentor luck.

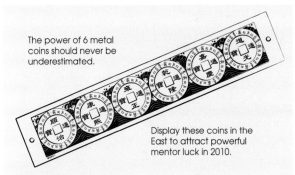

The power of 6 metal coins should never be underestimated.

Display these coins in the East to attract powerful mentor luck in 2010.

6 Metal Coins

It is incredibly beneficial to activate this auspicious star to benefit the whole household and this can be done by displaying **6 Large Smooth Coins** in the East. Doing so will ensure that everything moves smoothly. It is also a good way of attracting Mentor Luck to the household - powerful and influential friends who will assist you and open doorways to opportunities for you.

Updating Feng Shui

Updating feng shui is something that many wealthy and powerful families living in places like Hong Kong, Taiwan and now China arrange for without fail, each year. In recent years, the practice is also becoming increasingly popular in places like Singapore, Malaysia and Indonesia. Today, families consult feng shui retainers who use their expertise to insure homes against the intangible feng shui afflictions of the year.

These days anyone keen to do so can update their own feng shui. At *World of Feng Shui,* the annual feng shui chart is analyzed each year. This makes it possible for us to understand the nature and location of bad luck afflictions and good luck indications.

We explain the use of different remedies each year through our popular Feng Shui Extravaganzas which are live whole day events held in Singapore, East & West and Malaysia, the United States, the UK and in 2010, for the first time, also in French Polynesia! These events go a very long way towards protecting them against the year's afflictions.

The *Feng Shui Extravaganza* road show is takes place over 5 weekends before the lunar New Year, and is a wonderful way to connect with feng shui enthusiasts and to explain the fine points on what needs to be done each New Year. We genuinely look forward to doing these road shows. Those interested in attending any of our 2010 Extravaganzas, please note they are held in January and February 2010 and the dates and venues can be accessed at www.wofs.com.

Part 5
Improving personal feng shui

Each New Year, in addition to updating your space feng shui, it also benefits to make some adjustments that update your personal feng shui too.

The practice of personalised feng shui takes into account your animal sign as well as your individual Kua number.

You need to make adjustments to your facing directions and sitting locations to accomodate the different energies of the Tiger Year; thus your lucky and unlucky directions as indicated by your Kua number must be fine-tuned to counter the year's afflictions.

Remember that in using your lucky directions, you must always be mindfully aware of the influences of various annual afflictions. Even when a direction is generally very "lucky" for you, if in the Year of the Tiger that direction is negatively affected in any way, then you must NOT face that direction. Annual energies usually override Kua number lucky directions. Thus if your love direction is afflicted this year, then it is best not to activate romance luck this year.

Personalizing your feng shui makes a big difference to improving luck especially in a year as challenging as the Tiger Year 2010. Using your birth Lo Shu number to see how it combines with this year's Lo Shu number 8 also offers some interesting feng shui nuances for you to work with.

Finetuning Your Personal Directions

The compass based method of using your Kua number to determine if you are an East or West group person, and also for finding out your lucky and unlucky directions, is one of the easiest ways to practice and benefit from compass formula feng shui. Once you know your lucky directions, all you need to do is to arrange your home and office, and the furniture within, in a way which enables you to always face at least one of your good luck (and unafflicted)

Lo Shu & KUA Numbers for the Ox

Birth Year	Element Ox	Age in 2010	Lo Shu No. at Birth	KUA No. for Men	KUA No. for Women
1937	Fire Ox	73	9	9	6
1949	Earth Ox	61	6	6	9
1961	Metal Ox	49	3	3	3
1973	Water Ox	37	9	9	6
1985	Wood Ox	25	6	6	9
1997	Fire Ox	13	3	3	3

directions. Just doing this will immediately make a difference to your luck for the year.

The formula identifies 4 different kinds of good luck and 4 severities of bad luck, with each being represented by a compass direction. The 4 good directions allow you to choose a direction that brings you success, love, good health or personal growth. The formula also identifies 4 kinds of misfortune directions, describing the nature and intensity of each of these bad luck directions.

Once you are aware of your misfortune directions, systematically change your sitting and sleeping arrangements so you never face or have your head pointed to any of the bad luck directions. Feng shui is really that simple!

Don't forget to finetune the lucky and unlucky directions! Here are 3 things you musn't forget to take account of each New Year:

• Check whether any of your lucky directions are afflicted by any of the afflictive stars of the new year. This requires you to study the afflictive stars and afflicted directions laid out in the previous chapter.

• Take note of your own animal sign compass location and ensure that this location is properly activated and kept free of clutter, even if this is not one of your lucky directions. Remember that animal sign indication of direction overrides Kua directions! Your animal sign direction (which in the case of the Ox is NE1) is always lucky for you irrespective of what the Kua formula indicates. It overrides the

Kua formula but if the direction is afflicted by a bad number star for the year, then the location and direction should be avoided.

In the Year of the Tiger, the NE is afflicted by the Illness Star 2, so to be on the safe side, it is better for West group male Ox not to face the NE or sleep with their head pointed to the NE.

• Look at your Lo Shu number at birth and see how this interacts with the Lo Shu number of the year, which is 8.

Find out whether any of your lucky directions are in any way affected by bad luck stars during the year. Every year, the direction of misfortune-bringing afflictions change location, so it is vital to make sure that any lucky direction you may be facing is not afflicted in 2010. This is because time sensitive annual afflictions exert greater strength than personalized directions. Indeed annual energy flow usually possesses greater impact even than Period energies. **Time dimension feng shui affects the luck of the world more strongly than the space dimension of feng shui.** Only when you practice your feng shui with this particular awareness will you get the most out of feng shui.

Good & Bad Luck Directions for Ox

KUA Number	3	6	9
Success Direction	South*	West	East
Love Direction	SE*	SW*	North
Health Growth	North	NE*	SE*
Personal Growth	East	NW	South
Bad Luck Direction	SW*	SE*	NE*
Five Ghost Direction	NW	East	West
6 Killings Direction	NE*	North	SW*
Total Loss Direction	West	South*	NW

Note: All directions that are afflicted in 2010 are marked with * when a direction that is lucky for you is afflicted, you are recommended not to sue that direction this year. When the direction afflicted is one of your bad luck directions, then you must extra certain you do not get hurt by either facing this direction or occupying this location in your home or office.

Male and female Ox born people belong to both East and West group directions as their Kua numbers are 3, 6 and 9 for both men and women. The table to the left summarizes the good and bad luck directions for the three Kua numbers 3, 6 and 9.

To Activate Success Luck

Your personalized Success direction is your *sheng chi* direction. If you can face your success direction without being afflicted in any way by the annual afflictions then success luck flows smoothly, bringing advancement, growth and enhanced stature in your professional life. But you MUST make sure your Success direction is not afflicted.

Success Luck for Ox Born People

KUA Number	3	6	9
Success Direction	South*	West	East
Five Ghost Direction	NW	East	West
Total Loss Direction	West	South*	NW

For 2010, all Ox who belong to Kua 3 have South as their *sheng chi*, and this is afflicted by the 3 star which brings quarrels, court cases and terrible misunderstandings. For you, it is better to give the South a pass this year and face East instead, as East has the auspicious energy of heaven luck.

Look at your success direction for those born in the Ox Year summarized in the table above and you can systematically investigate which are the directions that are absolutely taboo for you. Facing either bad luck directions or afflicted directions will have an adverse effect on your success luck. If you really have no choice and cannot change your facing direction at work, even when the direction is afflicted, then first assess whether it is your Success direction that is being hurt and if so, how strong is the affliction. In this case, only Ox with Kua 3 are affected and here the affliction is the number 3 star which can be easily overcome by placing the **Fire Sword** or **Fireball** in front of you.

Kua Number 3

Male and female Ox with Kua number 3 belong to the East group and for them, their *sheng chi* success direction is afflicted by the hostile star 3. This indicates that should you face your success direction in 2010, your success luck is blocked by misunderstandings and arguments which could also lead to litigation. This year requires a great deal of patience from you if you are to enjoy the success luck potential shown in your chart.

The 49 year old Metal Ox in particular must take heed of this advice as your Success Luck is not only extremely strong this year, it is the only positive luck indication for you, so you will need to do as much as possible to heed this advice. You must also use Fire energy to subdue the 3 star.

Success here means that your professional and working life goes smoothly during the year with few, if any hindrances. With cures in place, when severe arguments manifest, you can overcome them, and when quarrelsome people cause trouble, whatever negative efforts they cause cannot succeed. This leaves a smooth path for you to bring your projects to completion. This is what Success Luck means in feng shui!

Kua Number 6

Male and female Ox people with Kua number 6 have West as their success direction. You also belong to the West group. This is very auspicious indeed because the West direction brings many good things in 2010.

To start with, the West is the direction of the Rooster who is an ally of the Ox, so this is a good sign. Next, the West direction has two powerfully lucky stars brought by the 24 mountains. These are the stars of Big Auspicious, so facing the West brings a double benefit for Ox with Kua number 6.

For women, this means the 37 year old Water Ox lady whose Finance and Success Luck are also at excellent and maximum levels. In 2010, if you can face the West at work or when doing something important such as making investment decisions or negotiating some important big deal or signing a contract, it will be extremely auspicious indeed.

Facing the West enables you to activate your *sheng chi* and also bring you the help of your ally the Rooster, who, by the way is going through an amazingly great year in 2010. So it is a very auspicious direction and definitely worth your while to make an effort to face.

This same analysis also holds for 61 year old Earth Ox gentleman and 25 year old Wood Ox young man. Both of you have excellent Success luck indications in 2010 and with West being so suitable and not afflicted in 2010, this is the direction you simply must tap for 2010. The West direction is also visited by the triumphant winning star 1, which brings success over the competition. So there are many good reasons to face your *sheng chi* direction in 2010.

Kua Number 9

Those of you Ox who have 9 as your Kua number belong to the East group and for you, the *sheng chi* Success direction is East which in 2010 is very auspicious as it is visited by the celestially powerful star of 6 which brings heaven luck. The East is flanked by two other powerful stars, the Star of Golden Deity and the Tai Sui, the God of the Year. Thus cosmic energy coming from the East is extremely powerful in 2010.

It is a good idea for those of you with Kua 9, to try and sit facing the East direction. This means the 61 year old Earth Ox woman and the 25 year old Wood Ox lady. For you both however, note that the East is the direction of the Rabbit, so facing East suggests that you should ensure that you do not get into any kind of conflict situation with anyone born in the Year of the Rabbit. This will help you to ensure great success for the year. For men, it is the 37 year old Water Ox that benefits from the East direction.

To Maintain Good Health

These days, with international travel being so extensive and people around the world on the move so much, there is always the real danger of epidemics spreading across continents. Good health can no

longer be taken for granted and it is now advisable
not only to keep the energy of the home vibrant and
clean, you must also make certain that where you live
is always filled with a good supply of yang energy. It
is when chi energy is moving and not stagnating that
residents within enjoy good health.

A healthy home is where residents enjoy good
resistance against bacteria and germs and are not in
danger of picking up infectious disease. Thus good
health in feng shui terms means you should eat well
and auspiciously; and also live well with enough
exercise and with no mental stress. When you have
a good healthy environment, you are unlikely to be
vulnerable to illness.

Sickness in any home is almost always due to bad
feng shui and also because the house itself is affected
by illness star vibrations which are left unchecked, or
worst still, which flourish because the environment
within fosters it. When someone gets sick in any
household, the sickness energy is always infectious so
residents will get sick, one by one.

Apart from catching the bug from each other, this is
also due to the illness star somehow getting activated;
and then it affects everyone irrespective of which part
of the house you stay in. Afflictive star influences can

move from one part of the house to another if they are not strongly curbed at source. This means placing **metal cures** and the **wu lou** in the NE corner which this year is the source of illness vibes.

Good Health Directions for Ox

KUA Number	3	6	9
Health Direction	North	NE*	SE*
Bad Luck Direction	SW*	SE*	NE*
Six Killings Direction	NE	North	SW*

For those who want to capture your individual good health direction, you can sleep with the head pointed to your Health direction. This is said to be the direction of the "Heavenly Doctor".

The table on this page summarizes the good Health Luck directions for all Ox men and women based on their Kua numbers 3, 6 and 9. Note that all the three Good health luck directions have one affliction or other in 2010. Thus those with Kua number 3 have North as their *tien yi* direction and in 2010, North is the place of the three killings. Facing North may bring the doctor from heaven to you but for you 49 year old Metal Ox, please take note that the Three Killings in the North can be deadly and perhaps no match for the good doctor from heaven. Do take note that you also have a double X against your health luck so you will need to be careful!

Those with Kua 6 have NE as their health direction but this is in direct conflict with the feng shui chart of the year. Here it states that the illness star of the year is located exactly where the heavenly doctor is located for Kua 6 people. This affliction definitely makes it impossible for them to face this NE direction. This directly affects the 37 year old Ox lady as well as the 61 year old and 25 year old guys.

As for those with Kua 9 your *tien yi* direction is SE and this too is afflicted by the presence of the violent star 7. Thus 61 year old and 25 year old Ox ladies should avoid sleeping with their head pointed to the SE as doing so puts you in conflict with the year's violent and robbery star. This definitely does not bring good feng shui.

Becoming a Star at School

For the 13 year old Ox teenager, 2010 brings exceptional performance and success luck. For you the year will favor you with some triumphant moments even though your chi strength is at a weak level.

You can harness extra good luck by energizing your Personal Growth direction as this will attract the luck of good concentration for you each time you study, do your homework or revise for school and public examinations. If you can face your personal growth direction while studying at home, or when working on an assignment; doing your home work or even when sitting for an examination, it will bring amazing good fortune for you.

The personal growth direction for Ox boys and girls are East (for Kua 3), NW (for Kua 6), and South (for Kua 9). Of these three directions, note that the South is afflicted by the hostility star and this is not a lucky direction to capture. Both the East and NW are good directions for 2010 so they benefit those with Kua numbers 3 and 6. Thus for the teenager Ox, facing the East direction brings good luck, as this direction is not afflicted in 2010.

Attracting Romance

Personalized Love Directions for Ox			
KUA Number	3	6	9
Love Direction	SE*	SW*	North

If you are looking for marriage opportunities, you must be careful that you do not meet up with married people pretending to be single. **Be extra careful because the *flower of external romance* star is running amok in the Year of the Tiger.** This means the libido of married people, especially married men are at a high. Singles should thus be extra skeptical of new people coming into their lives, especially if they are actively using love rituals to attract romantic opportunities into their lives. Here are three ways to attract love:

1) First you can activate your personalized peach blossom luck. For the Ox, your peach blossom animal is the Horse. You should place a beautiful, expensive-looking Horse in the South location of your bedroom. The Horse is a very special creature in feng shui, so do look for a good-looking Horse to

attract a good romantic partner! Do not get a Horse from pavement stalls or flea markets where the energy they are absorbing is unlikely to be very good!

> 2) The peach blossom star lands in the North in 2010. This is a powerful love direction for activating marriage luck. So no matter your age, irrespective of whether you have been married before, this is the direction to activate as well if you wish to benefit from the year's romantic energies.

3) You can also sleep with your head pointed to your *nien yen* or love direction. This is shown on the table to the left for the three Kua numbers that belong to the Ox, ie 3, 6 and 9. The way it works is to encourage *nien yen* vibrations to enter into your crown chakra while you sleep, by sleeping with your head pointed to this personalized direction. However, for Ox people, all three possible *nien yens* seem to be afflicted in 2010. The SE is hit by the number 7 violent star, the SW is hit by the five yellow, while the North has the Three Killings. As such, this might not be the best way to activate for love and romance this year. If you do need to use this method however, make sure you have the adequate remedy depending on your nien yen direction and the affliction that particular direction is suffering from this year. For example, if

your *nien yen* is North and you choose to sleep with your head pointed North to activate love luck, then make sure you wear the remedy to counter the Three Killings chi that may then affect you. Or if your *nien yen* is SW which is afflicted by the Five Yellow, wear the **5 Element Pagoda** cure.

Interacting with the Annual Lo Shu Number 8

While the Feng Shui Chart of the year reveals the energy pattern of the year, bringing new energies to every house, these also interacts with one's personal Lo Shu charts. Every animal sign is influenced by three Lo Shu charts which are created using their birth Lo Shu numbers. This is not to be confused with the Kua numbers discussed earlier.

The table on the following page reveals the Lo Shu number of those born in the years of the Ox extracted from the Thousand Year calendar. Take note that the Ox's Lo Shu numbers are 3,6, or 9 which reflect a number from each Lower, Middle and Upper period in the feng shui cycle of three periods which covers 180 years. The three numbers form a *parent string combination*.

The Lo Shu number at birth offers clues to the personality traits of the Ox and how they interact with the current year's Lo Shu number of 8. They also offer clues and recommendations to improve the year's feng shui luck for the Ox.

Lo Shu Numbers and Auspicious Directions for Ox Men and Women

Birth Year	Element Ox	Age in 2010	Lo Shu No. at Birth	Auspicious Direction for Men	Auspicious Direction for Women
1937	Fire Ox	73	9	East, SE, North, South	West, NE, SW, NW
1949	Earth Ox	61	6	West, NE, SW, NW	East, SE, North, South
1961	Metal Ox	49	3	South, North, SE, East	South, North, SE, East
1973	Water Ox	37	9	East, SE, North, South	West, NE, SW, NW
1985	Wood Ox	25	6	West, NE, SW, NW	East, SE, North, South
1997	Fire Ox	13	3	South, North, SE, East	South, North, SE, East

Ox with Birth Lo Shu of 9
(affecting the 37 and 73 year old Ox)

SE	S	SW
8	4	6
7	9	2
3	5	1
NE	N	NW

This is the Lo Shu chart for the 37 and 73 year old Ox born person.

The number 9 is an auspicious indication which stands for future prosperity luck. The number 9 chart has no direct link with the year's Lo Shu number of 8 other than it follows from 8 thus signifying the immediate future. Ox people whose Lo Shu number is 9 can build on the year's luck to create something long term. Note that the number 9 in the centre of the chart causes the hostile number 3 to fly into the Ox's home location of NE. This is not a good sign as it suggests that hidden hostility is being directed against you. So 38 year old Water Ox, you must be careful that you do not inadvertently offend someone. The 3 here when combined with the illness 2 of the year's chart is not a good sign for the Ox as this means the year's energy is exhausting the Ox.

Ox with Birth Lo Shu of 6
(affecting the 25 and 61 year old Ox)

SE	S	SW
5	1	3
4	6	8
9	2	7

(E on left, W on right; NE, N, NW along bottom)

This is the Lo Shu chart for the 25 and 61 year old Ox born person.

The number 6 is an ally of the number 8, both being white numbers. The number 6 indicates good strength. The element of 6 is Metal while that of 8 is Earth, so the year tends to exhaust the Ox whose Lo Shu number is 6. Note also that the NE sector of the Lo Shu chart has the number 9 when the centre number is 6. The two stars 9 and 2 strengthen the illness vibes in the NE. So those with Lo Shu 6 should strengthen their anti-illness cures in the NE. You will also benefit from wearing the **Antahkarana ring amulet** to ward off illness.

Ox with Birth Lo Shu of 3
(affecting the 13 and 49 year old Ox)

SE	S	SW
2	7	9
1	3	5
6	8	4
NE	N	NW

E ... W

This is the Lo Shu chart for the 13 and 49 year old Ox born person.

The Lo Shu number of this Ox has a Ho Tu combination with the year's number 8. Here the Ox 3 is Wood while the year 8 is Earth, putting the Ox in charge. The Ho Tu combination is also auspicious, definitely bringing success luck. This suggests that the year can be an exciting one for this Ox born.

Safeguarding Ox's Location
Use a compass to determine the Ox direction of your home which is NE1. This refers to the NE sector of the whole house and the NE corner of rooms you frequently use, such as your bedroom or your home office. You should make sure the toilet, store room and kitchen of the house are NOT

located in the NE1 direction. If they are, it will create a serious feng shui problem for you.

> A toilet in your Ox direction flushes away all the luck of residents belonging to the Ox sign. Career luck is hard hit and recognition will be blocked. Those in business face an array of problems including financial loss. A store room here locks up all your good luck. You will find it hard to fly and ambitions will get stalled. A kitchen here suppresses all your good luck.

If you envisage staying in the same home for several more years, it is advisable to consider changing the room usage of your NE sector, to create an active space where most of your productive work gets done. This energizes your most personally important sector of the home thereby benefiting you. Always make sure the energy here is vibrant and active, yang in nature and never has a chance to get stale for yin chi to accumulate. Changing the usage of the room is thus beneficial.

The Illness Star 2
In 2010 the whole NE sector is afflicted by the Illness Star 2 which brings misunderstandings and quarrelsome energies. You should thus examine

whether the affliction in this part of your house
or in this corner of your important rooms is made
worse by the presence crystals and other Earth
element objects as this will strengthen the illness star
considerably. Misfortune luck associated with illness
can be tragic so it is vital to keep the illness star
properly and adequately subdued.

The best thing to do is place Metal energy in the
NE as this will exhaust the Earth energy of the
illness star. Another great idea is to place a **Medicine
Buddha** image here as this brings in a celestial
remedy that is spiritually powerful as well.

The feng shui remedies that suppress the Illness
Star 2 are best placed in the NE of every room.
This affliction affects everyone who stays in the NE
room, but illness to Ox born people can be quite
severe if they are unlucky enough to catch it. So here
prevention is better than cure.

Improving your Door Feng Shui

One of the best ways of improving your feng shui in
any year is to ensure that the doors you use daily into
the house, into your bedroom and into your office are
auspicious for you. To determine the best direction to
use, we always look at the four auspicious directions
using the Kua formula of directions.

Auspicious Door Directions for Ox Men

Birth Year	Age in 2010	Element Ox & Kua No.	Best Door Direction	2nd Best Door Direction
1937	73	Fire Ox 9	East	SE
1949	61	Earth Ox 6	West	NE
1961	49	Metal Ox 3	South	North
1973	37	Water Ox 9	East	SE
1985	25	Wood Ox 6	West	NE
1997	13	Fire Ox 3	South	North

You can check the tables on this page and the next, then use a compass to determine the facing direction that works best for you, for each of the doors you use most frequently. Be very mindful about the doors you walk under each day. Making sure the doors bring good luck for you, however, is only the first step in improving your feng shui. It is also important to check if the facing direction of the door is afflicted by the year's energies.

Auspicious Door Directions for Ox Women

Birth Year	Age in 2010	Element Ox & Kua No.	Best Door Direction	2nd Best Door Direction
1937	73	Fire Ox 6	West	NE
1949	61	Earth Ox 9	East	SE
1961	49	Metal Ox 3	South	North
1973	37	Water Ox 6	West	NE
1985	25	Wood Ox 9	East	SE
1997	13	Fire Ox 3	South	North

For 2010, all doors that either face, or are located in the SW, NE, South, North and SE are afflicted and will respond positively to antidote remedies.

Below we give a list of the correct remedies which you can place either above the door, or flanking it. The more frequently you use the door, the more important it is to place these remedies. The doors referred to also include doors inside the home. These remedies do not send out harmful chi the way the Pa Kua with yin arrangement of trigrams do. (In the past, the Pa Kua was the only "cure" known and sold, and many used them indiscriminately, without realizing the potential harm they can cause.)

The remedies recommended here correct and subdue afflictions without creating bad chi. For all main doors going into the home, it is an excellent idea also to place the **powerful mantra plaques** in red because the mantras not only keep all bad vibes out of the house, they also bless everyone who walks under them.

-   **For Doors Facing SOUTHWEST**
    place the **five element plaque** above the door.
-   **For Doors Facing NORTHEAST**
    place the **wu lou door hanging** by the side of the door.
-   **For doors facing SOUTH**
    place the **kalachakra mantra plaque** above the door.
-   **For Doors Facing NORTH**
    place the **three celestial guardians** flanking the door.
-   **For Doors Facing SOUTHEAST**
    place **blue Rhino/Elephant door plaque**.

Blue Rhino and Elephant door plaque.

Use a good reliable compass to determine your facing direction of all your doors and make sure you stand just in front of the door to determine this. Do note that even when the "door" you use to enter the house is from the garage, and it is only a small side door, it is still very important.

Special Enhancers & Amulets for 2010

To ensure stability of luck for your household, it is an excellent idea to activate the center of the home, or at least the center of your living room area with a **crystal globe** containing **blue colored water**. We have designed a very special globe in two sizes – a 3 inch diameter globe and a six-inch diameter globe that is embossed on the outside with the 12 animal signs of the Zodiac. The globe is an excellent enhancer for the center number of 8 because this is an earth number.

The Earth element also signifies wealth luck in 2010 so the presence of a crystal globe here is very auspicious. Do try to twirl the globe daily to imbue it with yang energy. The water inside symbolically brings much needed water element into the living area. This is because the paht chee chart shows us that Water is terribly lacking in 2010.

For the Ox person, it is an excellent idea to place an Ox image next to the globe, letting it face NE. This creates good energy for your animal sign and should you so wish, you can also place your secret friend the Rat, as well as your allies, the Rooster and Snake. This will create excellent friendship energy bringing harmony and balance into your life. Special note for Ox – please note that both your allies have excellent luck this year, so stick close to them!

Special Talismans for the Ox

In 2010, the Ox person benefits from the following cures and talismans:

• A **Metal Wu Lou** to subdue the illness star of 2010. The Ox is vulnerable to physical and health ailments this year so it is good to wear protection. This is particularly important in the months of February, May, July and December.

Place this beautiful Wu Lou with powerful mantras by the side of your bed to ward off illnesses.

• Carry a **pair of Pi Yao** as a jade hanging, and display a pair in your home. The Ox sign is inconvenienced by the side Tai Sui in 2010. Having the celestial Pi Yao near you will ensure you don't suffer the wrath of the Tai Sui and instead, receive his support through the year.

• To overcome the side Tai Sui affliction, you can also wear the **Om Tare Tuttare Ture Soha necklace** in 18K gold. This is the mantra of the Goddess Green Tara and believed to clear all obstacles and overcome all problems for you.

• The **Namgylma Stupa** to protect against misfortunes and fatal accidents. Namgylma is the powerful Goddess of Longevity with 3 faces. She is also known as Ushnisha Vijaya. Her image and mantras that surround the stupa protect against premature death and natural disasters. She also brings wonderful new meaning into your life, surrounding you with an aura of great happiness. Displaying her Stupa in your home brings protection as well as happiness and contentment.

Namgylma Stupa.

• Wear a **Medicine Buddha Dzi bead** strung with blue obsidian. This Dzi will protect against sickness and strengthen your immune system. As your health luck is afflicted this year, wearing this Dzi will help ensure you do not catch any virus or illness that can develop into something serious.

• Display the **Bejewelled White Dzambala** in your home or on your office table. Keep this powerful wealth-bringing Deity near you to ensure you make the best use of the Star of Big Auspicious which you enjoy through the 24 Mountains.

• Get a **Fan with Omani mantra** on it to ward of infidelity dangers in your marriage. Ladies keep this inside your bag and use it as often as you can. The star of external romance is prominent in this Tiger Year, so those of you who are married should not take chances.

Fan with Omani Mantra

The 24 Mountains in 2010

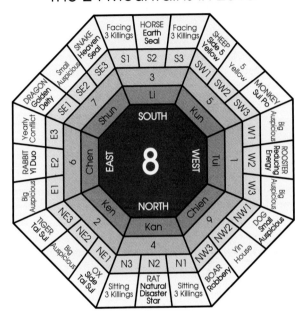

The number 8 dominates the year 2010 bringing auspicious energy to the Tiger Year. The 12 animals signs play host to the stars of the 24 mountains. These indicate the kind of cosmic forces influencing the luck for the year.

WANT TO LEARN MORE?

Don't Stop Now!

We hope you enjoyed reading your own personal horoscope book from Lillian Too & Jennifer Too. You are probably already feeling a difference in your life and enjoying the results of actions you have taken!

So, What's Next?

LILLIAN TOO'S FREE
Online Weekly Ezine NEW!

It's FREE! The latest weekly news and Feng Shui updates from Lillian herself! Learn more of her secrets and open your mind to deeper feng shui today.

Just go online to www.lilliantoomandalaezine.com and sign up today!

LILLIAN TOO's FREE NEW
Online Weekly Ezine!

Don't Miss Out! Join thousands of others who are already receiving their **FREE** updates delivered to their inbox each week.

Lillian's NEW Online FREE Weekly Ezine is only available to those who register online at www.lilliantoomandalaezine.com